LINCOLN CHRISTIAN

P9-CFZ-170

TAKING FLIGHT WITH CREATIVITY

WORSHIP DESIGN TEAMS THAT WORK

LEN WILSON & JASON MOORE

Abingdon Press
Nashville

TAKING FLIGHT WITH CREATIVITY
WORSHIP DESIGN TEAMS THAT WORK

Copyright © 2009 by Len Wilson and Jason Moore

All rights reserved.

No part of this work may be reproduced or transmitted in any form or by any means, electronic or mechanical, including photocopying and recording, or by any information storage or retrieval system, except as may be expressly permitted by the 1976 Copyright Act or in writing from the publisher. Requests for permission should be addressed to Abingdon Press, P.O. Box 801, 201 Eighth Avenue South, Nashville, TN 37202-0801 or permissions@abingdonpress.com.

This book is printed on acid-free paper.

Library of Congress Cataloging-in-Publication Data

Wilson, Len, 1970-
  Taking flight with creativity : worship design teams that work / Len Wilson and Jason Moore.
     p.   cm.
ISBN 978-0-687-65733-9 (pbk. : alk. paper)
  1. Public worship. I. Moore, Jason, 1977- II. Title.

BV15.W55 2009
264—dc22

                                                          2008047590

Scripture quotations are taken from the Holy Bible, NEW INTERNATIONAL VERSION®. Copyright © 1973, 1978, 1984 by International Bible Society. All rights reserved throughout the world. Used by permission of International Bible Society.

09 10 11 12 13 14 15 16 17 18—10 9 8 7 6 5 4 3 2

MANUFACTURED IN THE UNITED STATES OF AMERICA

ACKNOWLEDGMENTS

We celebrate both the times we have struggled to get off the ground and the times we have taken flight in worship design. Our journey has only been possible because of many fellow designers with whom we have planned worship over the last decade and a half.

We got our start at a church called Ginghamsburg United Methodist Church, in fields not far from where the Wright brothers did their work in Tipp City, Ohio. To the teammates of our first experience taking flight, we thank you. Thanks for becoming iron sharpening iron, for nurturing space to dream and freedom to fail, and for the faith you all showed in the power of designing worship as a team. None of us could have known the impact now of what we were doing then. It was a gift to have served with you.

Despite flying so high, we felt God calling us to step outside our church to better assist other local congregations with creative ministry. So we started working on another plane. After earning wings, we thought taking flight with a new team would come easy. It didn't. We'd guess that the Wright brothers had to face bitter cold, equipment failure, and damaging winds to achieve their feat. We question whether our adverse conditions were even worse. Without the drive and determination of teammates Tom Boomershine and Amelia Cooper, we would have certainly stayed on the ground. Thank you for your prayerful approach to team, your willingness to come back to the table after a crash, and for your continued friendship. We achieved much together as Lumicon. More importantly, we learned much with and from you.

To our extended family at Church of the Resurrection in Leawood, Kansas, we want to extend huge thanks. What started as a three-day consultation has grown into a true friendship over the past few years. Working on worship design with you has been a joy, and we look forward to future collaborations.

Together we've consulted with several church teams as part of our ministry at Midnight Oil. These experiences have contributed and shaped many critical ideas. Thank you, to each of these worship teams.

Jason would like to thank the Livingwater United Methodist Church design team for trying so many things that seemed far beyond what a little church meeting in a YMCA could accomplish. Those meetings and the resulting services were so much fun and such a blessing to so many. God bless each of you in what you're doing today in ministry.

Len would like to thank Dr. Stan Copeland and the Crosswalk worship team for taking in a homeless worship designer and letting him stink up the little room with the big table at Lovers Lane United Methodist Church in Dallas, Texas. What a great space for worship we had there, and how much fun we had in using it.

"There's no place like hope" is more than the motto of Community of Hope United Methodist Church in Mansfield, Texas. It's the truth. As I discovered, it's a different aeroplane altogether to design creative worship for a church plant meeting in a high school cafeteria. Thank you, Joe Carmichael, for your willingness to try team again after my begging and pleading. It was exciting to help you, the worship team, and the congregation of COH bridge the transition to your own space, and it has been a joy to watch you grow.

And to Len's current team at Trietsch Memorial United Methodist Church in Flower Mound, Texas, consisting of John Allen, Paul Bonneau, Karen Chraska, Frank Hames, Traci Henegar, Kris Melvin, Alan Miles, and Randee Paraskevopoulos: I have never felt more useful in ministry. Thank you for your positive spirit and your eagerness to try fun stuff just because we can. May God bless our team and our church.

Last, Jason dedicates his efforts in this book to his daughter Madeline Darby Moore, who entered this world just around the time this book was being finished. Your smiles warm our hearts, and we're so excited to see what God has in store for you. Love, Daddy.

And Len dedicates his efforts in this book to Austin Wade Wilson, his little smiling face of joy.

CONTENTS

Foreword. vii

Introduction ix

**Part 1: Are We Meant to Fly? Discovering a Strategic
Approach to Worship**

Chapter 1: Why Design Worship in a Team? 3

Chapter 2: Identifying Team Purpose 9

Chapter 3: Addressing Issues of Methodology 17

**Part 2: Building the Aeroplane: Putting the Worship Design
Team Together**

Chapter 4: Who's on the Design Team? 25

Chapter 5: What's the Size of the Design Team? 31

Chapter 6: How Does the Team Operate? Team Equality 35

Chapter 7: Who Does What? Team Roles 39

Chapter 8: How Do We Organize Our Time? 49

Part 3: Taking Flight: Achieving Koinonia

Chapter 9: Becoming a Small Group 59

Chapter 10: Learning to Make Decisions Together 69

Chapter 11: The Weekly List of Decisions 79

Chapter 12: Brainstorming 93

Chapter 13: A Worship Case Study 99

Part 4: Grounded: Dealing with Team Maintenance and Problems

Chapter 14: Sole Proprietor Preachers 107

Chapter 15: Maintaining a Finely Tuned Machine 115

Notes   125

FOREWORD

The church today faces the challenges of an ever-increasing multi-ethnic society, technology, urbanization, as well as race and class disparities in such areas as education and employment. How will the church be relevant in the midst of all this, that people might come to know Christ personally as well as find a Christ-centered mission for their lives? The church must strive like never before to be relevant. It cannot afford to stay grounded in segregation, extreme traditionalism, and isolation from the culture around her. The church must take flight!

I love the metaphor Len Wilson and Jason Moore use in this much-needed book and the opportunity it gives the church to be multisensory and relevant, and to engage culture for Kingdom purposes. Len and Jason are using their gifts to equip the church to excel in its evangelism. They are truly two gifted young men with a heart to see the church take the risk of combining technological tools with authentic reconciling relationships so that the church might be salt and light.

I had the privilege of serving on staff with Len and Jason at Ginghamsburg United Methodist Church when I was there in the late 1990s as a youth pastor and back-up preacher to the senior pastor. I became a better preacher as I met with a worship design team to share what God had put on my heart. I was stretched by the diversity and gifts of that team. This creative approach to worship design also became an experience in racial reconciliation. Because as an African American I was on a team with people unlike me, my sermons became a combination of my authentic background combined with others on the team. The time we spent in prayer, brainstorming creative and crazy ideas, was an experience of worship and community in and of itself.

Now a senior pastor in Minneapolis, I look forward every week to meeting with our worship design team. I look forward to it because at the end of the day I want to participate in a weekly worship experience that is bigger than me. I want the weekly worship experience to be bigger than my preaching, bigger than my gifts, bigger than my ethnicity, and bigger than my gender. This creative team approach has led our congregation to launch a Hip-Hop worship experience, a worship experience that focuses on compassion, mercy, and justice, and a worship experience that is multi-ethnic and intergenerational. It has also led us to engage more people in our congregation to serve in areas of their passion and gift set.

The church must be willing to be creative and embrace change so that it might truly see deep life transformation. For the church to be innovative in this way, we have to be open to reexamining not only our experiences of corporate worship but also our leadership structures and our core values. There are church leaders who will read this book and be ready to change the Sunday morning worship experience but may be hesitant to truly empower staff and laypeople around them to assist in shaping that experience. This book calls us to more than just putting on a cool worship service. It calls us to rethink organizational structures, and it pushes senior pastors to check their egos in order to build a team that will wrestle with what God wants to say and to utilize multiple gifts of those around us that God might stay strong. If the church refuses to heed the call of this book, instead of being salt and light, she will be a tasteless and dying institution.

A creative, team-oriented approach to worship design can be about more than just what happens on a Sunday morning. I've found in my experience that it can truly be a journey of reconciliation and intimate community development. I'm not just excited about what this approach has done for our congregation, but for what it has done within me. This approach has assisted in further crucifying my flesh that I might fly. Don't just read this book so that your church can take off and go to the next level. Allow it to speak to you in a deeper way, so that it will take the potentially grounded life of a leader and cause it—through the power of the Holy Spirit—to soar among the clouds.

Efrem Smith
Senior Pastor, the Sanctuary Covenant Church, and Author of *The Hip-Hop Church* (with Phil Jackson, InterVarsity Press)

INTRODUCTION

Flight is an enduring human desire. For most of history, to soar above the earth like the birds of the air has been confined to the stuff of imagination. The disappointing chasm between dreams and the reality of human flight had eluded scientists, engineers, and dreamers for millennia, from Ezekiel's wheel to Leonardo da Vinci's sketches to Octave Chanute's failed tests of 1894.

Two brothers from Dayton, Ohio, also had the dream of manned flight. It began as a boyhood fascination with a toy "helicopter" and ended up becoming one of the most inspiring stories of innovation and triumph ever told. Orville and Wilbur Wright changed the world on December 17, 1903, on a fittingly named area of grassy sand dunes in North Carolina called Kill Devil Hills.

A great sense of personal accomplishment in solving the mysteries of flight must have fueled their passion for finishing their mission. Later, they may have marveled at the impact their ragtag operation would have on culture in the early 1900s. Yet, they never really got to see how much they changed the world. In fact, it is almost impossible now to grasp the magnitude of what these men, working as a team of two, accomplished. The passage of time, along with descriptions and dramatic recreations of these events, have colored their story in ways that make it impossible to fully capture what happened. But this much is clear: it is impossible that the Wright brothers had any idea of the global impact their discovery would have. Human flight, as much as any invention or discovery before or since, ushered in an age of globalization. Their influence can be seen from the dirt runways in third-world countries to the most state-of-the-art airports in the biggest cities in the world.

Why were the Wright brothers able to take flight, while others had failed? We believe the key lies in their relationship. Whereas many of their predecessors had more resources, education, and support, nearly all of them worked on the pursuit of flight alone. It would seem no coincidence that Orville and Wilbur succeeded where so many others had failed and that they were co-collaborators working as a team. For more than one hundred years now, we've been in the air because two kindred spirits led the way in the discovery of something neither could have accomplished alone. The sum total of their feat equaled more than their two parts could have achieved individually.

We got our start in ministry in Dayton, Ohio—the same town where the Wright brothers began their journey toward the sky. It is hard to miss their influence when literally walking down the same streets and looking up at the same sky that they dreamed of soaring through. Their father was a bishop in the United Brethren in Christ denomination, an ancestor denomination to the congregation we initially served, Ginghamsburg United Methodist Church. We have long been inspired by the Wright brothers' story, and have found some great insights for ministry in the iconic tale of their vision and innovation. As we take a look at teams, and the challenges associated with creating successful ones, we'll continually look to the Wright brothers' partnership and the metaphor of flight as a way to understand and help create worship teams that work.

PART ONE

ARE WE MEANT
TO FLY?

Discovering a Strategic Approach to Worship

Whether humankind was meant to fly was a topic of some debate at the time of the Wright brothers' accomplishment. Similarly, the extent to which a strategic team should plan and design worship is a matter of some debate today. If worship teams are to get off the ground, they require a sense of purpose and calling. There cannot be questions about their existence. This section looks at strategic approaches to designing worship in collaboration with others.

CHAPTER ONE

WHY DESIGN WORSHIP IN A TEAM?

L et's just be honest here and admit it: our worship stinks." Those were the words of a denominational official, addressing a group of pastors and other church leaders at a meeting on congregational growth and development. We were pleasantly surprised at his candidness. He was being brutally honest, but he spoke the truth. Good worship is a compelling, powerful, life-changing experience; yet so often what we create on Sunday morning falls far short of this potential. Instead of taking flight in worship, we stay on the ground.

For some, the inability to fly is tied to the denial that such flight exists. There's an old saw that states, "If man were meant to fly, he would have been born with wings." In all likelihood that pithy zinger fell out of the mouth of a naysayer at the turn of the twentieth century—someone who had never seen or experienced flight and assumed it didn't exist. Maybe it was someone watching the Wright brothers or others of their ilk crash a crazy flying machine with four sets of wings into a house or barn, like in an old Buster Keaton film clip. That person looks the fool now, assuredly. To mix a transportation metaphor and quote Francis Bacon: "They are ill discoverers that think there is no land, when they can see nothing but sea."

Similarly, there are Christians who—in a lifetime of church attendance—have rarely if ever known a powerful, transformative experience of the Holy Spirit in a corporate body of fellow believers. These people are often victims and sometimes perpetrators of a variety of dysfunctions that keep them grounded.

We believe it is possible to take flight weekly—to design and experience transformative worship on a regular basis. And the way to consistently achieve flight with creativity is through the work of a team of collaborative worship designers. But first, it is important to look at what worship is, theologically and methodologically, and why teams should be a part of its design and creation.

Defining Worship

Do you ever feel effective worship is something other people do and have? Do you feel like you're grounded in the same old holding patterns while those around you are soaring to new heights in creativity and power? Sometimes our best efforts seem to go nowhere, or even worse, end up crashing in a big heap. While others fly ahead we find ourselves covered in dust and beaten up by our humble attempts at effective worship.

This book is for people who remember why they got into ministry in the first place—people who do the work of creating corporate worship because they want to see other people encounter a holy and living God, and through that encounter experience healing and transformation. This book is for people who believe and hope that worship can be a truly transformational experience. It is not about creating worship that is doctrinally or historically correct, personally edifying, "nice" (like Milquetoast), entertaining, or even aesthetically pleasing. It's about worship that works.

What does that phrase mean, you ask? We believe worship works when it is the basis for personal and social transformation. Worship works when we—believer or nonbeliever, saint or sinner—meet God through the Holy Spirit, and in that encounter confess our brokenness, discover God's grace, and are made new.

Further, the experience of worship, or maybe we should say the "noun" of worship (as opposed to the "verb" of worship), is the primary vehicle through which, on an everyday, local level, we demonstrate on a corporate level what it means to be a Christian. When people worship (verb) together in corporate worship (noun), transformational things happen.

We don't believe that worship is limited to acts of glorification or adoration, although they are certainly a part of the worship experience. Good and true worship forms the basis for discipleship and social transformation. It is out of worship and the Christian community within which it occurs that personal and social change happens. Worship is the core of the church. It is the single most important, recurring reflection of the body of believers. It is the big gathering. It is "prime-time" Christianity, if you will.

Bells may be going off in your head with that last statement. "Whoa! Worship is not a production!" you say. This is true. Worship supersedes any understanding of an experience rooted in words like *program* or *event*. Such a shallow interpretation misses the point of planning a corporate gathering in the name of Christ. Choreographed cultural spectacles are a dime a dozen, and certainly the Holy Spirit appears in even the least organized of gatherings. Effective worship of any sort is separate and distinct from what we may call the "wow" experience. It points people in powerful ways to the risen Lord.

Yet at the same time that worship is not a production, or more than the summary of its technical components, it is indeed a production, worthy of our best planning and effort. The presence of the Holy Spirit is not an excuse for the absence of creative vision or any sense of forethought. On the contrary, the Holy Spirit is often found moving in places with the highest creativity and best organization. For if we don't use our creativity to plan worship that engages and moves us, then how can we expect it to move others? Fumbling through a mediocre service can impede the work of the Spirit, whereas creatively planning a smoothly flowing worship experience allows us to "get out of the Spirit's way" as it moves in people's lives. That doesn't just happen by creating a song list and a standard three-point sermon. It takes hard work. This book is about designing worship that works.

Designing Worship

How do we, as twenty-first–century proclaimers of the gospel, enable our worship to take flight?

We suggest one key way is by establishing effective worship design teams. Emphasizing teamwork and teams-based organization has been trendy in corporate culture for a while now, to the point where *Saturday Night Live* has parodied the irony of ragtag corporate groups of coffee drinkers in crumpled shirts sitting around a featureless conference room table, with a big, supposedly inspirational banner proclaiming "Together Everyone Achieves More" behind them on the wall.

As followers of Christ, however, there may be more to teams than meets the corporate eye. True teams of people, operating as two or three gathered together in the name of Jesus, doing ministry together, know something that mere money-makers cannot: the power of the Holy Spirit. This kind of community is known as *koinonia*, a Greek term found often in the New Testament. To coin a simple definition, based on the different ways it is often translated into English, koinonia is the intimate fellowship of sharing, participation, and contribution that followers of the risen Christ experience.

Although it is incredible to experience, koinonia is more than a feelgood moment. To quote a song by the band R.E.M., it is more than "shiny happy people holding hands." Koinonia has power. It does something. It is the dynamic of a community of believers out of which amazing things happen.

Case Studies

We know this at more than a theological level. We know it because we have witnessed it firsthand at churches we have served over the years. When a group of Christians set aside themselves and set about the work of the Kingdom, truly amazing things happen. We believe in the power of worship design teams because we have lived it, first in an amazing period of growth at Ginghamsburg United Methodist Church.

Ginghamsburg is a large, influential congregation in rural Ohio whose rapid growth and pioneering style of worship began to draw national and international attention in the mid 1990s. Len served as the first media minister there, from 1995–2000, and Jason served as the church's first full-time artist from 1997–2000. During this period, worship attendance tripled to more than three thousand attendees weekly. Much has been documented about Ginghamsburg's innovative model for designing worship (see Kim Miller's *Redesigning Worship*, Abingdon Press, 2009), and we could spend a book dissecting and understanding the innovations that occurred during that late-1990s period alone. But since that time, a myriad of additional experiences in churches of a variety of sizes has broadened our scope significantly.

After this seminal period, we worked together for two years on a parachurch team designing and sometimes implementing worship that had to work for churches spanning a large spectrum of sizes and styles. For another period of about two years, Len worked with a traditional "high steeple" church forming a worship design team to serve a new "contemporary" service. Jason served for two years with a team designing contemporary-style worship for a church plant that met weekly in a

YMCA and averaged about 150 in worship. Len then spent two years serving as a volunteer worship designer for a small but growing church whose attendance grew from 150 to 400 during his time there. Since 2006, Len has designed worship with a team at a large church in the Dallas-Forth Worth area, Trietsch Memorial United Methodist Church.

In addition, we have consulted with a variety of congregations encompassing a variety of denominational traditions, sizes, and worship styles, and we have conducted short-term consultations at churches ranging from fifty to fifteen thousand in weekly worship attendance. Although this seems like a bit of a laundry list, it evidences that we have seen, in a variety of settings and with a variety of models, worship design teams that work—and ones that don't.

The Power of Teams

But what if you have never experienced amazing, transformational teams in ministry? What do you do then?

Take a glimpse at the working relationship of two brothers from the Midwest whose combined efforts went beyond what either could have achieved alone. The birth of flight was much less glamorous than myth may suggest. On the morning of December 17, 1903, at Kitty Hawk, North Carolina, Orville and Wilbur Wright put a plane in the air for twelve seconds, covering a total of 120 feet. That's ten feet per second, or 6.8 miles per hour. They probably could have run faster. But by the end of that same day they had launched three other flights, with the last going 852 feet in 59 seconds and ending in a dramatic accident that nearly totaled the plane and ended test flights for the rest of that year.

Their feat was remarkable in ways that we probably can't fully imagine. It literally took years of blood, sweat, and tears just to go 120 feet in the air. The path to this victory wasn't smooth by any means. The Wright brothers took their victories however they could. It is important for us to view our struggles in ministry with teams the same way. There will be conflicts and failures, with tiny victories in between, but if we stay committed we can be assured that eventually we will achieve the sometimes seemingly elusive yet transforming sense of koinonia.

In *The Wired Church 2.0*, Len wrote, "Don't do this alone. Don't even try." Teams make organizational sense; but more importantly, they are the embodiment of Christ in the daily work of ministry. Many of us know this, at the business or theological level or both, and spend much time recruiting, training, and working with teams in our daily ministry efforts. But do we really practice effective teaming? Good teams should take us to heights unimaginable by ourselves. This is a product of not just a team but a team with koinonia. That spirit of koinonia creates team effectiveness that would be impossible if any one person attempted it. It is the purpose of having teams in the first place—the experience of being a part of something great. Koinonia is truly living as the body of Christ.

As a team of two who has also worked both individually and collectively with a number of other teams, we have learned a few basic principles for developing this koinonia in a worship planning environment. This book is designed to help teams of Jesus followers everywhere take flight with creativity and discover worship design teams that actually work.

IDENTIFYING TEAM PURPOSE

A s a word, *purpose* is on the verge of becoming a cliché. Rick Warren's famous book *The Purpose Driven Life*, one of the best-selling hardbacks in U.S. history, created an entire trend around the word, in church circles and in the culture at large. There are purpose-driven business models, purpose products and marketing campaigns, more purpose books, and even a Purpose Prize funded by the Templeton Foundation. As with anything of influence, there's also a thriving counterculture that opposes elements of Warren's approach, such as the idea of a causal purpose from God for every individual, or opposes the very framework for Warren's philosophy, which has been characterized as modern, linear, and out of touch with emerging ideas about community (pun intended).

Love it or hate it, one of the biggest problems we see in churches is a lack of purpose in worship design. Too often we see worship "on accident," rather than worship "on purpose." A root cause of this problem is the inability for everyone involved in worship planning to agree about the goals and direction for the church's worship service(s). In many of the consultations we do for local churches, we detect an unspoken disagreement about what worship is and for whom worship is designed.

Worship on Accident

Often, strategic decisions on a particular worship service occur by accident. Worship planners pay little to no attention to the "big picture" questions, and what happens in worship on a weekly basis becomes a reflection of the dominant personality or personalities in the planning process. Worship with a strong leader may function well in this scenario for a time, as the leader imbues the process with his or her individual theology and philosophical approach to worship. For a while this may seem like a workable, even ideal scenario. But dangers await. Consider several examples of the disasters that can befall congregations that approach worship with one leader's philosophy, rather than with an agreed-upon, overall purpose:

The leader leaves without a strong personality to replace him or her

Maybe you've witnessed this scenario: First Church has a contemporary worship service held in the fellowship hall. When the service first started, a charismatic singer with a guitar led it. Worship attendance grew as people were attracted to the singer's style and personality. But after eighteen months the singer vacated this role, without malice, when his wife finished her doctorate and they had to move. Without another equally charismatic personality to step in, worship seemed to lose its vitality, and attendance dropped precipitously.

A change in leadership

Consider a congregation that undergoes a pastoral change. The outgoing pastor had an outreach focus in worship, using the corporate gathering as a time to connect with the community and communicate using ordinary ideas, images, and metaphors. The new pastor has a discipleship focus and uses the corporate gathering time as the main venue for in-depth exploration of biblical texts. Such a dramatic shift can create immense tension and controversy in a congregation, especially when the shifts are not addressed.

Two leaders with conflicting philosophies

When the purpose of worship is assumed, major differences can lie below the surface, exploding like a bomb when someone innocently activates the tripwire with an inquiry about style. For example, the pastor views a secular song as an opportunity to engage the culture, whereas the worship leader plays it begrudgingly because it is not in and of itself a worship song. When a layperson inquires about the song's purpose in worship, it draws out unspoken tensions. This often manifests in the form of a pastor and a worship leader who have fundamental differences in worship that are never addressed.

The leader suffers a moral indiscretion

When a moral indiscretion occurs, the leader's worship philosophy, which has over time become a central part of congregational identity, comes into question as well, and the congregation may be tempted to "throw the baby out with the bath water." The congregation blames not just the leader, but also every change that leader brought, and suffers what can be a mortal wound.

Each of these scenarios is a real-world example. We've seen them happen firsthand. In each case, the results were disastrous for the worship service, the congregation, and God's Kingdom.

Worship on Purpose

The alternative is to design worship with purpose. It is vital for worship design teams to discover a common vision for worship design. A worship team with purpose comes to consensus about major directions in the service's theology, methodology, and style. The team also has an agreed-upon structure for how to design worship. A team with a mutually agreed-upon purpose is able to withstand each of the above scenarios, as it is not dependent on one person's charisma but rather on a grounded, prayerfully agreed-upon set of principles.

What are these principles? They fall into three main categories: worship philosophy, methodology and style, and team organization and structure. When teams work together to address these aspects of worship design, they will soon identify a more clearly articulated sense of purpose for worship in their congregation.

Worship philosophy

What does the team believe is the purpose of the gathering? This is the foundational question for any group of believers that wishes to gather corporately. Is the purpose of worship at your church adoration, discipleship, community, or outreach?

Avoid the temptation to say "all of the above"—not because you don't want to include all of these elements, but because you're deceiving yourselves if you think it is possible to do all four at once. It is akin to identifying a target audience as "everyone," when in fact a church will target a certain demographic, intentionally or not. Most of the time the target audience of a church is a "people like us" demographic; so if a church is

mostly white women over fifty, then that church's worship style and program offerings will feature the kinds of things that appeal to white women
over fifty. Similarly, a church's worship philosophy tends to reflect the
values of its leadership.

Whereas each of the approaches to worship outlined below may represent a valid expression, worship at every congregation takes on a certain
flavor. As stated, this happens on accident or on purpose. Think of a worship service in which you have been involved. Would you say that it was
stronger or weaker in certain of these areas? Was that merely a reflection
of the worship service's leadership or was there a clear sense of purpose
behind the areas the worship team chose to emphasize?

What do these four categories—adoration, discipleship, community,
outreach—represent? Here is a brief description of each. Note they are
not mutually exclusive, nor is one inherently superior to the others.

1. *Adoration.* The praise and worship movement has seen the
   rise of many megachurches with an emphasis on adoration in
   worship. Largely evangelical in heritage, many of these congregations have a focus on music as a means to glorify God.
   Many of the largest churches in America fit this model.
   Dallas-Fort Worth, where Len lives, is full of these kinds of
   churches. Churches with an emphasis on adoration might
   say, "Praise, worship, and adoration of the Creator is the
   focus of worship music." The implication is that the high
   point of the worship experience is the corporate gathering of
   a body of believers to glorify God.

2. *Community.* Mosaic, the Los Angeles church led by Erwin
   McManus, has become well-known for its emphasis on community. McManus took over a Southern Baptist church in
   East Los Angeles called The Church on Brady and has
   helped it grow, partly through worship with a focus on community. The church eventually changed its name to capture
   this new identity—a mosaic of believers all coming together
   as one body of Christ. Unusual for a Southern Baptist congregation, Mosaic serves Communion every week. The
   implication is that the high point of the worship experience
   is the Eucharist, the ultimate expression of Christian
   community.

3. *Discipleship*. The United Methodist Church of the Resurrection has become well-known for its emphasis on discipleship. Pastor Adam Hamilton has led what has become, according to *Outreach* magazine, the largest United Methodist Church in the United States. The church's approach to worship is classically Protestant, with an emphasis on teaching from the pulpit. Hamilton uses current events as a window to biblical truth in his sermons. The implication is that the high point of the worship experience is the sermon, or the proclamation of the Word, which in the modern era shifted from narrative to expository.

4. *Outreach*. Willow Creek Community Church, one of the largest and most influential churches in North America, became well-known for its effectiveness in outreach through worship, with its focus on creating an experience for "unchurched Harry and Mary," their imagined target, who are typical, upper-middle-class suburban boomers in the Chicago area. Outreach in the context of worship is alternately constructed as evangelism or mission. The implication is to engage the culture in the church's most visible time using everyday language and methods, as Jesus modeled through his own ministry, and is an extension of the sermon-centered approach to worship.

Churches with effective ministries often arise out of strength with one or sometimes two of these philosophies of worship. One real-life sample philosophy statement from a church that ranks adoration and discipleship as its highest priorities states: "Worship is about God and for believers." Another, from a church that ranks adoration and outreach and evangelism as its highest priorities, says: "Worship is about ushering people in to the presence of God." Two that emphasize community and outreach say respectively: "We desire to be a caring family of multiplying disciples influencing our community and world for Jesus Christ," and, "Our philosophy of worship at our church is that we are God's people sharing the love of Christ."

Which of these four approaches describes your church? Rank these four philosophies of worship in order of importance for your service. You may find your order is different for different services your church offers. Your traditional service might emphasize adoration and discipleship, whereas a more informal service might focus on community and outreach. A greater self-awareness of your congregation's philosophy of worship allows it to be more strategic in its direction. For example, a church whose worship identity is strongly tied to community and discipleship can stop debating the various options and design worship strategically focused on building up a body of believers through community and discipleship. Similarly, a large church seeking to create an alternative service may consider creating an identity that is opposite to the main service in order to connect with those in the body marginalized by the main service's "feel."

Individuals on the worship team may each have their own unique approach to worship. That is fine. The key is to collectively decide what worship for the congregation is, philosophically, and what the team wants worship to be. Teams with a unified vision will find the work of worship to be much smoother. Frank Hames, a member of the Trietsch Memorial UMC worship team, says, "The most powerful element of our team is a common vision of what great worship is. There are many components to excellent worship and this team is on the same page with most of them. When we are striving to germinate an idea, I feel like we are going in the same direction. When someone has a great idea, the consensus is usually unanimous."

Methodology and style

We have discussed worship methodology in other writings, particularly in chapter 5 of *The Wired Church 2.0*,[1] "Concurrently Cultural and Countercultural," and we will focus on it in more depth in the next chapter. The point to emphasize up front, however, is that every worship service has a particular methodology. It is impossible to remove cultural and historical context. There is no answer to the question, *Why can't we just forget all of this stuff and worship God?* Every church must decide on its own where to position itself on the cultural continuum, from "traditional" congregations that continue to practice eighteenth- and nineteenth-century methodologies to "contemporary" and "alternative" congregations discovering innovative, fringe methodologies to "emerging" congregations who are looking to the ancient past for what are once again fresh methodologies—and everything in between.

Methodology is an extension of philosophy. For example, a service with an emphasis on outreach might be eager to embrace the latest methodological models, such as what is sometimes called "experiential worship,"[2] out of a desire to connect with people unmoved by tradition. A discipleship-oriented service may not need to be quite so concerned about such trends. Style stems from methodology and refers to music and the arts, to visuals and creativity, to preaching, and to use of participation and interactivity.

Consider these two examples of a statement about methodology, found on actual church websites:

> The purpose of worship arts is to utilize a variety of art forms during corporate gatherings to provide an atmosphere conducive to the working of the Holy Spirit. Believers and unbelievers alike should be provided with an opportunity to hear the powerful truth of God's Word in a culturally relevant way, and be encouraged to seek, serve, and worship our awesome God.

> Our worship sees all communications media, including spoken, written, and digital forms, as equally important in sharing God's love. Since, in Jesus, God is no longer behind the Temple curtain but out in the street, both sacred and secular music may be appropriate forms of worship.

Be careful to differentiate between philosophy and methodology. Consider this statement: "The purpose of the Worship Arts Ministry is to bring glory to God through the arts and lead the congregation to become free to worship in exaltation." This is a philosophy statement with a nod to methodology ("through the arts"). Try to be more exact.

Team organization and structure

Clear-eyed and frank discussions on how the team is to function is important for warding off future conflict. These can be related to individual commitments, meeting details, and even to how the team intends to handle disagreements and work together. Statements detailing the team's commitment to meet regularly, arrive on time, and fully participate in designing weekly worship services may seem too obvious to mention. Chances are, they'll become valuable later. Here are a few more real-life examples.

> Our team agrees to remain fully committed to the worship development process through its duration.

Our team is not a committee, which operates without actual hands-on involvement in its decisions, or a task force, which exists for a limited time, but is an ongoing group of people, intimately involved together.

Our team agrees to address interpersonal and ideological conflicts openly and in attitude of prayer and exhortation, rather than ignore or avoid them.

Although the purpose statement doesn't need to be treated as a legal document, the more specific it is up front, the better the team will be able to focus on creativity and the movement of the Holy Spirit, rather than getting bogged down in a mire of confusion.

ADDRESSING ISSUES OF METHODOLOGY

Landfills of books have been written about the "worship wars." Maybe they're called wars because there are so many casualties. The goal of this chapter is not to add to the carnage of the worship wars, which most people have declared over (though some traditionalists fight on, like Japanese soldiers on isolated islands after World War II). Rather, our goal is to help deconstruct the loaded language in play—first, in our presumptions about worship style, and second, in our theology of Word. Worship design teams must dissect and understand these methodological issues before they can make critical decisions on strategic direction.

Deconstructing "Traditional" and "Contemporary"

Recently we were speaking at a large conference on worship, and the speaker who preceded us made a statement that really caught our attention. He said that although the church has spent much time, effort, and energy creating contemporary worship services, it has simply created new forms of traditional worship. "Think about it, folks. The root of 'contemporary' is 'temporary,'" he said.

Those words rang in our ears. If one believes, as we do, that worship should connect with people of this time and space, both believers and unbelievers, then we have to have a "temporary" mind-set. Although the presence of God in Christian worship is timeless, the methodologies we use to increase our own awareness of this presence should be ever changing. The Spirit will always be moving in our lives and in our churches, so we have to stay fluid in our methodologies. We should stay true to our core values, while changing our cultural practice. This is the true purpose of contemporary worship.

There is irony in much of what is currently known as contemporary worship. Many congregations have a vague desire to create contemporary worship (that is, a style of worship more contemporary than what they already have) but don't have a clear direction about what exactly it is that they hope to accomplish. Often what results is a specific style of worship that is structured around the tastes of those creating it. The style then grows old with its designers. It becomes fossilized. What is still called "contemporary" is no longer contemporary at all.

What does it mean, then, to be "temporary" in worship? What is true contemporary worship about, exactly? The root of *contemporary* is *tempus*, which is Latin for *time*. The adjective derivative of this root is *temporal*. *Temporal* is defined as "relating to measured time" or "lasting only a short time."[1] This is not a very apt description of the worship style we often call "contemporary."

As one aspect of worship, consider musical styles. Contrary to much of what is practiced, worship is far more than just singing; but it can be a good place to start. For many, poor-quality music or even high-quality music from a bygone era results in an inability to be aware of God's presence.

Many contemporary-minded music ministers believe that for the most part traditional hymnody doesn't easily connect with or inspire those who haven't grown up in the church. Even for some who have, it can be a difficult task to connect to God through this type of music. What some music ministers fail to see, however, is that often older contemporary worship music is to the new generation what hymns were to the generation that first shifted away from hymns. Some of the classic songs of the contemporary repertoire such as "El Shaddai" by Amy Grant or "Great Is the Lord" by Michael W. Smith were written thirty to forty years ago. They are two generations old to young worshipers today. Choices made by music ministers have to be thought through carefully if the goal is to connect worshipers with an experience that is not stale, but is instead relevant to the current time.

Consider yet another definition of *temporal*, which has roots in our Christian tradition: "relating to the laity rather than the clergy in the Christian Church."[2] In other words, to be temporal in worship means to connect with the people in the seats—to speak their language and not the language of the clergy. Many pastors and worship leaders I know have a set of musical tastes that may or not may not match the tastes of their congregation. It is important when designing contemporary worship to consider laity musical styles.

As ministers, we should be as intentional as Jesus was about how we communicate the gospel. The problem with much of traditional and contemporary worship is that it tends to alienate people. If the worshiper— believer or nonbeliever—doesn't know the esoteric response lines or the significance of certain objects or words, or even the appropriate behavior, then he or she is lost. We speak a "Christianese" language without even knowing it sometimes. Many hymns and liturgical writings have language that needs significant deconstruction to even begin to understand what is being shared. This is true regardless of the style of worship.

Our worship design emphasis, therefore, is not to create esoteric worship that speaks exclusively to a ruling class in the body of Christ, who are privy to the mysterious code of "Christianese," but to create worship that is an expression of the entire body of Christ—the everyday person. The essence of the Incarnation is that Jesus came to Earth to make God's love possible. God became human for everyday people so that we, as these people, can find a connection with a wholly other God. Jesus exclusively used stories from the culture and metaphors (parables) from his day to teach. He rejected the rhetorical style taught in the Temple. His ministry was to those outside the walls, not the ruling religious class; his language matched that style of ministry (Mark 4:33-34).

A third definition of *temporal* is in opposition to *eternal*, that is, "connected with life in the world, rather than spiritual life"[3]; in time rather than out of time; "in this world," to use Jesus language. As believers, we know that life in Christ is ultimately not of this world. It is timeless. The kingdom of God is both now and forever—the very opposite of temporary! It is often tempting when in God's presence for us to want to just pitch a tent and hang out on the mountaintop like the disciples at Jesus' transfiguration (Mark 9:2-13); to be disconnected with things of this world. Jesus calls us to come down off the mountain, go into the world, and preach the good news (Mark 16:15). The disciples didn't pitch a tent and hang out on top of the mountain. Jesus sent them back down to minister, to proclaim the gospel in their own time. We must do the same— not being content to live out of time, but living the temporal life for the sake of bringing others along. Even as we follow a Savior not of the world, we must stay connected to life in the world. For contemporary worship designers, this means the focus is to continually design worship that is truly contemporary, or connected to the world.

As the church moves further ahead in time, much of what is now known as contemporary will become traditional, and what is now known as traditional will no longer exist. This cycle of innovation and institutionalization is typical. To much of the broader culture, worship that becomes institutionalized or "set in stone" is seen as an attempt to hold on to the past—whether meaningful or not. This form of worship continues to speak to a certain (small) demographic, but its rituals and language often prevent genuinely searching people from experiencing God.

For contemporary worship designers, the move from archaic forms of worship to methods that are more connectional, using present cultural communication forms, has to be considered if the church is to move forward in its mission to make disciples. We should strive to create worship environments where our members can feel comfortable inviting everyday people—our neighbors, literally (many of whom are very much of this world); where when they walk out the doors of the church with their guests by their side, significant deconstruction of specific words and rituals are unnecessary; where the words that they sing, the message they hear, and the images they see connect to their personal experience.

To live this mission means that our understandings of worship should constantly change. We must continually come down off the mountain. We must guard against pitching the tent and exhort one another to keep those at the bottom of the mountain in our hearts. Truly committing to connect with the culture through worship, then, may mean that contemporary 1970s worship with acoustic guitars and "Kum Ba Ya," contemporary 1980s worship with a lot of synthesizers, and contemporary 1990s worship with that familiar grunge sound might need updating. The way the church does worship today *should* look different than it did five or ten years ago. It should continue to look different in the next five to ten years too. Our ministry at Midnight Oil is devoted to helping churches stay *of this time*, while following whatever direction God may take us. We are committed, as the church should be, to changing with the culture for the sake of making disciples.

Reassessing Your Theology of Word

Mark 4 tells a story from the early part of Jesus' public ministry in which Jesus tells the parable of the sower. It's a long parable, the longest in the Gospels (vv. 3-9). Afterward, when the crowds had left and the disciples were alone with Jesus, they revealed to him that they had no clue as to what he had been saying. Possibly frustrated at their lack of understanding, Jesus took the time to explain the entire parable to them, actually spending more time on the explanation than he had on the parable itself (vv. 10-20).

Instead of concluding that such a creative presentation of the gospel didn't work and returning to the religious rhetoric he had demonstrated in the temple (Luke 2:41-52), he continued to speak in parables, telling the parables of the lamp on the stand (Mark 4:21-25), the growing seed (vv. 26-29), and the mustard seed (vv. 30-32). "With many similar parables Jesus spoke the word to them, as much as they could understand. He did not say anything to them without using a parable. But when he was alone with his own disciples, he explained everything" (vv. 33-34).

Parables were Jesus' exclusive public style! He didn't simply use parables as an alternative for the stupid ones in the crowd. Metaphorical teaching was his only public method. Jesus understood that to communicate ideas effectively, he had to present his teaching in a medium that made sense to his audience. People in our time still listen best when spoken to in a familiar language. That language changes over time, and those in ministry must change with it.

Look even across the span of time in which the Bible was written. In the Old Testament days, the word of God was something spoken; it was oral. It was God's word. In the beginning, something was true or real because God said it. God said, "Let there be light," and there was light. People of faith passed down the stories of their experiences with God through a vibrant oral tradition.

There is a shift in this over the course of the Bible's story, as writing became more prevalent. By the end of the Bible's story, something is true or real because it is written. At the end of the last Gospel, John writes, "But these are written that you may believe that Jesus is the Christ, the Son of God, and that by believing you may have life in his name" (John 20:31). This written culture continued for centuries, exploding even more with the invention of the printing press. From the Reformation until just recently, the written word dominated in worship (prayer books, hymnals, reading manuscripts for sermons, and so on).

The word of God is no longer just oral; it's not just written, either (commence throwing stones). So what is it?

Well, the beginning of John's Gospel provides some help with the famous lines: "In the beginning was the Word, and the Word was with God, and the Word was God.... The Word became flesh and made his dwelling among us" (1:1-14). The Word, then, is not spoken or written; it's personified. It's Jesus. This is a radical line in the Bible.

To proclaim the gospel—or as some would say, "teach the Word"—in worship, really means to proclaim the person and story of Jesus Christ. Teaching the Word is not merely to engage in an expository deconstruction of text. That's a modern-era approach tied too closely to "Word as text," or thinking of the little *w* instead of the big *W*. Although the words of God as contained in the Bible tell us of Jesus, the Bible is not the object of our faith. Jesus is. The Bible points us to Jesus. Our goal is to proclaim Jesus, and him crucified and resurrected from the dead. It's the living, risen Lord. That's the Word. And we can tell it through oral means and written means; and we can also tell it visually, through art and symbolism, through participation, and so forth. Each one of these media may be sanctified through the telling of the story.

This theological issue is apropos to any discussion about how to communicate in worship. The church's understanding of Word is shifting—or at least the text boat it rides in has sprung a few leaks in this digital era. This is happening everywhere—to congregations of all theological persuasions as they begin to use visuals in worship. It's the old axiom that what we communicate and how we communicate are intertwined.

How does all of this apply to designing worship in teams? Just as an individual pastor must have a theological and philosophical foundation for ministry, the team must have a foundation that forms the basis for its methodological direction. If the team is stuck in "Word as text," for example, it will find itself facing many obstacles to the implementation of creativity, image, and art. Although there are of course other theological considerations in worship, these two—the "contemporary" question and the theology of Word—are in our opinion two of the most relevant questions for teams to consider as they form a common strategic direction.

BUILDING THE AEROPLANE

Putting the Worship Design Team Together

The ongoing work of a worship team offers both opportunities and obstacles to success. Answers to every decision, from who is on the team to what their roles are, from how big the team is to how it operates, can separate worship design teams that fail from ones that work.

WHO'S ON THE DESIGN TEAM?

U nlike planes on today's modern runways, the Wright Flyer didn't take off from a smooth, paved surface. Before the first flight test took place, Wilbur and Orville worked in the bitter cold to lay one hundred feet of track on a smooth stretch of ground. They meticulously measured wind velocity and compared it to data they'd been collecting for years in wind tunnel and practical glider tests. All this was done in preparation for what they hoped would be a successful run.

Though they probably didn't call it such, what they were creating was the first flight plan. With a preflight checklist in place and a theoretical system for landing the plane devised, they felt comfortable moving forward. Had the track been haphazardly laid or the wind speed not been measured, they very likely could have failed. Many pieces needed to be in place to make the first flight possible. The same is true with worship design teamwork. Putting the team in a position to fly takes much preparation and care.

Before entering ordained ministry, Len's father was an infantry officer who served two tours in Vietnam. One of his favorite sayings is, "Mistakes in deployment cannot be overcome." In other words, many teams fail at the start because of bad choices made at the outset about who its members are. What are some of the characteristics of good worship design team members? Consider the following and choose wisely.

Plugged In

Do you know any digital thinkers? No, we don't mean people who think in binary code. Rather, who do you know who could be a spokesperson for what's current in culture? These are the sorts of people who follow the latest Web trends, such as social networking. They like to go to new releases at the movie theater. They seem to know a little bit about anything that's current. They're the kinds of people who dive into a new piece of software without timidly trying to read the manual first. These sorts of people are comfortable with new trends. They are less likely to suggest something just because it's been done before, and more likely to push envelopes of creativity, technology, and innovation. In our experience they are invaluable in their ability to add fresh ideas.

A Lot of Young People

Young people are great. We know; we used to be young people! Seriously, young people bring an enthusiasm and eagerness to do what's fresh. They're more likely to be free of the sorts of constraints that prevent new and creative thinking around worship design.

Young people, because of their lack of experience, are also more likely to try something unusual. They haven't been told often enough, maybe, that such an approach is a bad idea. We like to say that young people are willing to beat against the wall until it falls over. Older people can get tired of swinging. As Warren Bennis notes, "They don't yet know what they can't do. Indeed, they're not sure the impossible exists."[1]

In some churches we've visited, the fifty-year-old secretary is the young person of the church. If that's what you've got to work with, then go for it. Young is relative.

More Generalists than Specialists

The initial inclination may be to find the best specialist around, such as the savviest sound engineer, the best musician, or the coolest graphic artist. This may not be the ideal approach. Rather than filling the team with specialists who only speak to one area, it's better to look for generalists. Specialists may stay silent when discussing areas outside of their expertise; generalists know a little bit about many different fields and are more likely to comment on the general topic in a meeting, even if it isn't "their area."

This is vital to team collaboration. Having each specialist inform the team of his or her individual decisions on a particular service is not team planning at all. A church could handle that by e-mail. It is imperative that within each area of design, such as the musical selections, everyone on the team be able with some degree of knowledge to contribute to the discussion. This is the power of team planning—that exponentially more ideas emerge that wouldn't have been considered alone. Later, team members can take on specific roles within the planning process as their gifts apply.

Diversity

How well does the team reflect the congregation? It is important to find people who can speak with experience on the issues facing your church. For example, if you have a large group of twenty-somethings in your church, you'll want at least one articulate twenty-something on the team to discuss what that group is experiencing in life. Similarly, a church with a large graying population needs to have representatives of that generation on the team.

Even if your congregation is fairly homogenous, diversity means reflecting your target community's variety in age, race, gender, and cultural or political perspectives. Ideally, the team would be diverse in these ways too. Two of the teams we were on really benefited from diversity in terms of age, race, gender, and political views.

One of the passions at Ginghamsburg Church was and continues to be racial reconciliation. This meant that we not only wanted to promote the concept in worship, we wanted it to be reflected in our worship design. The exchange of cultural viewpoints often helped us identify issues that we likely would not have considered otherwise. On the same team, we had ages ranging from early 20s to mid 50s. This really widened the spectrum of ideas exchanged during the meetings, especially where music and movies were concerned. Both genders were present too, although males outnumbered females. This meant often that we'd have a more masculine slant during early brainstorming and our lone lady would have to work the room to bring us around. We would have likely benefited from a more even mix. Our Lumicon team didn't have racial diversity, but age and political diversity often helped us design worship with broader appeal. It was also the source of heated debate from time to time.

The tendency to want to find all like-minded, similar people might be strong, but we'd recommend trying to choose members who will represent a wide array of life experience and cultural background. With that stated, don't sacrifice team unity in order to create a brochure photo. Make sure the people you choose are fit for the task, committed to the task, and can "play well with others."

Strong Leadership

Leadership in a collaborative environment is a bit different from that in a typical hierarchical structure. In teams, leadership is function, not position. This means that the position of leadership means very little. In fact, the more the position of leadership is emphasized, the more that creates problems for the creativity of the team. A good team needs to feel organizationally flat—if not in fact, at least in effect.

For example, many successful teams we've been a part of or consulted with have assigned team leadership responsibilities to one or more other people besides the pastor. On these teams, the pastors are just members of the team, taking care of their responsibility to help direct the main idea and present the sermon. Another person, such as the team producer, runs the meeting (see the chapter on roles for more about that). It is hoped that everyone in the room is a leader as well, in charge of other people or tasks.

Bennis notes that effective teams "are almost never bureaucratic."[2] Hierarchical limitations and arbitrary boundaries don't apply. Individuals are liberated from an oppressive leader and are free to collaborate, dream, and create. In this environment, leadership is best given out in small, soft doses.

Plays Well with Others

Last, the ability to articulate a vision clearly and kindly is essential to good teams. A person can be the most creative mind in the room, but if he or she cannot express a vision in a way that makes sense and attracts others, then that person and others just get frustrated. We've seen this happen more than once!

Creative talent needs to be able to work well together. Good teams are not the place for the strong-willed and talented genius who sees a vision in his or her head and must manifest it exactly as it is visualized. Teams form collective visions and see them through as a team. Further, being able to play well with others is not the same as being pleasant. The greater prerequisite is to be mutually focused on the common goal. The character Cristina Yang on the television show *Grey's Anatomy* is a doctor in training who is part of a surgical team. She is intense and not amiable whatsoever. But her laserlike focus on the mission of medicine makes her an ideal teammate. The ability for team members to challenge status quo thinking, present a strong will, and offer new ideas are great characteristics for an effective worship design team.

One question we often receive in our seminars is, How do I find good team members? The above list of job qualifications is a start. More important though is a foundation that the church and its leadership sets. Sometimes great team members find you. Creative talent gravitates to a creative atmosphere. We often say that when you start implementing creative worship, you will be shocked at the people—and the number of people—who come out of the shadows to join in on the fun. Lay the groundwork for worship that works by demonstrating it. To paraphrase the oft-used cliché from the film *Field of Dreams,* if you build it, talent will come.

CHAPTER FIVE

WHAT'S THE SIZE OF THE DESIGN TEAM?

Just as important as who to choose in forming a worship design team is how many people to choose.

One of the hottest shows on cable television is the outlandish international reality series *Iron Chef* and its sister series *Iron Chef: America*. These intense culinary contests pit two top chefs against each other in a race against time to create flavorful and eye-catching recipes in a particular food category. The hook in each episode is a secret ingredient, which is dramatically revealed to the chefs at the start of the competition. This ingredient, which can be as radical as fish in the pastry category, must be a part of every item they are assigned to create in the one-hour contest.

Neither of the competing chefs works alone. Each has at his or her disposal a team of trusted assistants called sous chefs, who, under great pressure, must work together to create winning recipes.

Whether on *Iron Chef* or in your favorite restaurant, even the most talented chef could never do his or her job alone. Individual chefs could never meet the ongoing demands of a hungry restaurant crowd. Working with others encourages experimentation and continued learning opportunities. Good head chefs realize they can learn from their assistants. For example, sous chefs are typically assigned an area of the kitchen, such as the grill, where they are empowered to specialize in a particular skill. This affords them the opportunity to participate in the creative process, representing their specialization, while the chef is developing new recipes. A team of people working together is a must to achieve success.

However, maybe you've heard the old phrase "Too many cooks spoil the broth." It's a way of saying that too many people making decisions at once will bog down the process and inhibit both creativity and productivity, making the experience miserable for everyone. Those who have prepared a big meal for family holiday gatherings may know the truth behind this saying. Just as it's necessary for people to work together, it's also possible to get in one another's way.

There are a lot of parallels between preparing food and worship. Determining how many should be in the kitchen will affect how well the meal comes out. Too many, and nothing gets done, but not enough and a lot of opportunities are missed. An ongoing struggle for many congregations concerns the size of the worship design team. What is an ideal number? We have seen teams of all sizes, from two to twenty and even more.

Is it possible to design worship in a team of two? Sure. The Wright brothers were a team of two, and they did a pretty good job designing the airplane. We know of one two-person worship design team that was successful for a number of years. But in a team of two, the process is more difficult than it needs to be. One reason is that there are fewer people to fill the necessary roles each team must have.

This is a key distinction to make. Good worship teams are not driven by specific personalities but by fulfillment of specific roles. In general, the more team members who are capable of fulfilling multiple roles, the better off the team is. Cross-train team members to fulfill as many roles as possible. In general, this enables you to decrease the size of the team. Small teams can overcome a lack of bodies in the room if the few that are present can each accomplish many tasks. There will be more on these specific roles later.

Of course, we'd recommend more than two people on a worship design team. Just as in the kitchen, more people on a team make for a greater diversity of viewpoints and evaluations. As we frequently say, alone, a bad idea is a bad idea, and designers often don't know it's a bad idea until it is on stage, when it's too late. In a team environment, a bad idea is a launching pad to greatness—the more team members are present, the more likely one suggestion will lead to another, better suggestion.

In our own experience, instead of creating teams that are too small, the tendency for many congregations regardless of size is to attempt to operate with worship design teams that are simply too big. We have seen this repeatedly. This was the case in our initial worship team environment at Ginghamsburg. When Len joined the team it had been functioning for a few months, at least in name. It had not yet begun to take flight, however, because it suffered from the Knights of the Round Table disease.

This particular malady occurs at many medium and large congregations. When a new team is formed for the purpose of meeting with the senior pastor, whom we'll call King Arthur, to design worship, every department head, or knight, wants to come to the table as an expression of power in the politics of the kingdom of the congregation. This list may include the small groups pastor, the discipleship pastor, and so on. The sickness occurs when the knights refuse to lay down their swords—which happens more often than not. The resulting environment is not teamlike at all but rather a succession of talking points. The "Knights of the Round Table" don't listen but instead just wait for their turn to speak. Their conversational goal is to shift the agenda toward decisions that favor their own turf.

Big teams skew toward a diversity of viewpoints that have difficulty coming together. Consensus, not compromise, is vital in a team. Even without the Knights of the Round Table disease, big teams simply have too many opinions. This is to say nothing of the challenge of big teams having enough roles for everyone to serve a purpose.

We consulted with a large church once that had more than fifteen people on its design team. We never got an exact count of the team's size. When we discovered this, we about had a coronary! "How in the world can you design worship with that many people?" we asked. The answer was, they couldn't. Eight months after the consultation, we received an e-mail saying they had restructured their organization. The new worship team has five people.

This is well within the target, as research studies on brainstorming have shown that the best teams range in size from four to seven. Fewer than four puts a greater onus on the skills and gifts of a few people, which makes finding team members very difficult and burnout more likely. More than seven people in a room together makes it difficult for everyone to feel a part of the discussion and feel ownership of its results.

One last thought about team size: some churches, without acknowledging or intending it, operate with a worship design team numbering in the hundreds or even thousands. Whereas feedback is necessary for teams to stay connected to the congregation, be careful about allowing too many layers of influence. The entire congregation cannot design worship.

Congregations of different traditions have varied organizational structures, both staff and lay, but regardless of the environment within which your team operates, it is important to protect the creative process. It is the job of the team, not of vocal naysayers, to design worship. Most churches struggle with more than a few creative opinions in the room at once. Imagine the strain of multiple unseen forces attempting to influence design as well.

HOW DOES THE TEAM OPERATE? TEAM EQUALITY

One of the most influential books of this young century has been *The World Is Flat: A Brief History of the Twenty-first Century* by Thomas L. Friedman. Friedman's analysis of globalization includes ten "flatteners," the most disruptive of which he says is "open sourcing," or the shift from the power of an individual to the power of a community.

Friedman argues that the twentieth century demonstrated the power of the individual, as mechanization and communications technology allowed one voice to be heard not just locally, regionally, or even nationally, but globally. Individual voices became very powerful, from authors and artists to CEOs and heads of state. Although the ability for an individual to exert great power has occurred throughout history, in the twentieth century there were more people of power on a bigger world stage who crossed greater geographic and cultural boundaries—from heads of state like Lenin, Roosevelt, and Hitler to businessmen like Henry Ford to media moguls like David Sarnoff and Rupert Murdoch. The consequences were dramatic.

Now, though, digital communications is giving voice not just to individuals with great charisma and singular visions but also to anyone with technological savvy, an opinion, and the recognition of a few others. Technology, more ubiquitous and democratized, has begun to enable great numbers of people to form groups of voices. Labeled the rise of the "niche" in some business circles,[1] Friedman calls the phenomenon "uploading." The rapid rise of social networking websites such as Facebook and MySpace and collaborative knowledge sites like Wikipedia is an easy indicator. Facebook encourages members to waste countless hours linking themselves to groups of people with common interests and traits such as "falls asleep easily."

But there is more to uploading than that. For example, the increased threat of terrorism is perpetuated by groups of like-minded people adhering to a single idea. These groups are collectively more terrible than the power of any single member, using flattening technology to enact dark visions. But just as this phenomenon is not all sweetness and light, it is also not all gloom and doom. Flattening forces are greatly contributing to the rise of living conditions for large portions of the world's population. Millions in China and India, for example, have begun to experience opportunities for their young people not only to get an education but also to use it in their own country.

In Western countries, uploaders are everywhere, irrespective of age, gender, socioeconomic status, or any modern inhibitor. But what does uploading have to do with ministry?

Uploaders for Jesus

The modern, twentieth-century model for ministry, riding the wave of new communications technology, gave rise to über-pastors—from Billy Graham and Robert Schuller to Rick Warren and Bill Hybels; individuals with great influence; church equivalents to great heads of state. These über-pastors continue to have great exposure. But as tenets of modernism continue to fracture, the future of the church, particularly in the daily life of an ordinary congregation, is in community.

You want a team that actually works? Forget the pastor as control center. Team equality is key. Find a team of uploaders who want to change the world with the good news of Jesus Christ. This is the essence of Paul's exhortation in 1 Corinthians 12—the priesthood of all believers acting as a body with Christ as the head.

The flatter a team can function, if not in fact then at least in effect, the better off it will be. As stated, in worship design teams that actually work, leadership is function, not position. Vertical structure hinders creativity. If a supervisor is in the room with those designing worship, individuals, especially if they are creative spirits, may feel inhibited and find themselves focusing more on political dynamics than on creativity. For most, even greater than the desire for creative expression is the desire for self-protection. Given the choice, someone will usually hesitate to speak a new idea, especially one that might be considered close to the edge, if there is a possibility that that idea may hurt his or her position on the team or even in the congregation.

Further, creative people expect to contribute in this age. Teams that work allow empowerment, because creative people won't hang around an environment where they are told, explicitly or implicitly, what to do. This means that those in the highest positions of authority need to minimize their role for the sake of allowing the team to flourish and allowing creativity to take root, even if the initial consequences are frightening.

Pastoral Leadership

The notion of team leadership for worship may be scary to some pastors. We are not advocating that the pastor abdicate his or her position of authority or saying that the position of leadership, such as a senior pastor, is not important. Consider the biblical metaphor of shepherd, which encourages pastors to assist in the qualitative task of the growth of the flock, unlike the secular metaphor of CEO that is focused on achieving quantifiable metrics such as numbers in worship, new programs, and giving levels. The point is that hierarchical teams (or those perceived to be by their members) simply don't work. Later on, we'll discuss the pastor's role of providing theological leadership and direction in a collaborative environment.

As one church-planting pastor reflected to us:

> I remember in our early days, a consultant spoke of us being a motor-boat, not a ship. Our structure allowed us to make quick turns and changes. I realize as an organization grows the more prone it is to lose its "flatness." However, I trust that we will be able to maintain some of it, especially in the area of creativity.
>
> I'm uncertain if most pastors are able to step away from the "hierarchical" role and allow others the freedom of creative expression. Nevertheless, for a creative team to operate to its maximum potential, there must be a sense of a level creative field. That means all team participants, pastors included, who choose to explore this "flat team" creation effort need to kindly unhook from their own sense of importance and leave it outside the door before stepping into the process.

Contrary to the perception of many, in this age of corporate transparency a pastor who utilizes a team is not weak but is instead an effective leader, functioning as a member of Christ's body, with Christ as the head.

Further, good teams support pastoral leadership. Again, look to the story of the first flight. Many less-heralded parties, including technicians and engineers, were part of the team that got the first plane in the air. For example, the Wright Flyer flew because it had an engine turning the propellers. It left the ground because it had traveled down a one-hundred-foot-long track, building up the needed lift to fly. Few know the name of bicycle shop employee Charlie Taylor, who built the engine for the Wright Flyer, yet he was an essential part of the team. Lifeguards John T. Daniels, William S. Dough, and Adam Etheridge aren't household names either, but they were part of the five-man team (the other names weren't even recorded) who carried the six-hundred-pound plane to the runway track before it began its journey. In the end, the Wright brothers couldn't have made history that day in Kitty Hawk alone, but popular history would credit the brothers as working alone. In the same way, the pastor gets the "credit" when worship takes flight, necessarily reinforcing his or her position as the leader of the congregation. Effective worship, when a reflection of the work of a vibrant flat team, does not diminish the authority of a pastor; it enhances it.

CHAPTER SEVEN

WHO DOES WHAT?
TEAM ROLES

Each Sunday, sports fans all across the country crowd around television sets to watch one of America's favorite pastimes: professional football. Why? Maybe it's the food or the fancy uniforms, or maybe it's just the thrill of watching a group of men function as a unit.

Whether in last place or first, no team would dream of taking the field without a plan in place. Players don't wait to decide who's taking what position when they huddle up for the first time on the field. Each role is defined long before the season starts. They train hard together, and when they've done their work and know their role, on game day when the whistle blows each player is free to have fun doing what he does best. Knowing what job to do and how to execute it is what makes teams work.

If your worship design team were about to play the big game, would you know what your position is? What about the others on the team? If your team has no game plan, you may find yourselves running in circles, and most likely finishing with a losing record.

Game plans don't just come together. They are the result of a group of players, each with defined roles, working out their designs ahead of time. This can be a difficult process. As opposed to the veto power one planner has when creating worship in isolation, working in a group of people is not as easily controlled. As in every small group, dynamics evolve. Some individuals who are more introverted in nature may stay quiet in the midst of brainstorming and interaction. Others may gravitate toward different functions that suit their giftedness.

Team roles are one of the most important aspects of team development. Whether putting together a brand-new team or working with one that's been in place a while, roles need to be defined in a way that every participant understands.

Why Are Roles So Important?

Disgruntled players are often ones who don't feel their contributions are being acknowledged. They feel they don't have a vital role to play. When everyone feels ownership, individual agendas become team agendas. When individuals are able to drop their own preferences and focus on what is best for the team, the first step to a functioning team occurs.

Roles also help in the creative process. When roles are clearly defined and understood, teams are freed up to focus on creativity and brainstorming, and not on who is doing what for each meeting. In our experience in worship team planning, once roles are defined there is often a noticeable sentiment of relief felt within the team regarding how the brainstorming will translate to the service being implemented. In other words, no one is worried that all of the creative stuff is going to get lost or forgotten once the meeting is over, because each person knows what he or she is responsible for.

Assigning roles to everyone on a team is necessary to ensure avoidance of the dreaded "peanut gallery," where some members of the team implement the ideas generated in a planning meeting and other members get to shoot holes in their creations at the next gathering. We have seen more than one team suffer because of this dynamic when some people have specific roles and others don't.

Be cautious, though, about roles becoming a roadblock to creativity. Every role or area of responsibility must be seen as an area of leadership where others are welcome to give input. People who function in these roles should not act as gatekeepers, making decisions in an area of expertise whether an idea is acceptable or not. The group decisions of the team must supercede individual preferences. We'll have more on the gatekeeping problem later.

Team Roles

So, what are the roles? The makeup of your team's roles may vary according to your own unique context, but here is a starting point for thinking about the specific needs that must be present in a worship team.

Roles are not people. Some teams can have two or three people filling all of the necessary roles; other teams can have as many as ten. If your team is the ideal size of four to seven people, each will serve at least one of these roles and some will serve at least two.

Preacher

Obviously, a preacher is on a team to fulfill the duties of preaching. But in a worship team the preacher is not necessarily the de facto team leader. We have witnessed multiple successful teams where the preacher has handed team leadership responsibilities off to another person. In Len's current team at Trietsch Memorial UMC, senior pastor John Allen defines his role as restricted to "theme selection and scripture interpretation."

Every team needs to have a preacher. This may seem like a no-brainer; but we have witnessed many teams attempt to function without one. Some preachers, citing other demands on time, will send notes to a meeting in lieu of themselves. One team's preacher did just this, saying that he had an important small group meeting to attend, so the notes would serve as a proxy, of sorts. The team planned as usual, without their pastor's presence, developing concepts that made sense in the context of their brainstorming session. But the next Sunday morning, when the preacher saw the image the team had designed on screen, he was confused, saying he had no clue what it meant and couldn't integrate it.

The team tried again the next week without the preacher's presence, and when he saw the image the following weekend he adamantly refused to use it, saying it represented a concept that was directly opposed to his intent.

After two consecutive failures, the team's preacher realized his presence was necessary for the team to function well. He realized that, simply put, pieces of paper don't talk back. In a brainstorming session it's necessary for the seed ideas to be represented and healthy dialogue to occur around them, and for the one doing the preaching to be present in order to elaborate on his or her ability to integrate the concepts into the message.

A team may also consider having a second preacher on the team. Let's assume the first-string preacher intends to take a vacation or two at some point in the year. What happens when the back-up preacher enters the mix? One without any team knowledge seriously hinders the ability of the team to do its job, but a back-up preacher who has been on the team is able to fill the role without too much disruption in the development process. This second-string preacher will also want to assume another role on the team to avoid joining the "peanut gallery."

Bandleader

This person is the head musician and represents all of the musical portions of the worship experience. He or she is an absolutely critical part of any functioning worship team. Since music is such a large and vital part of most worship services, musical choices that don't fit what the team designs can disrupt the entire planning process.

We've seen much resistance from musicians in the past to allowing others to participate in the song selection process, but this is an obstacle that must be overcome. Ideally, a creative team designing one cohesive service would choose music that complements the theme for the day. If the service focuses on purity, then songs of purity (such as "Create in Me a Clean Heart") make more sense than songs of adoration (such as "Shout to the Lord"). Utilizing all of the team members in the selection process makes for a wider array of choices.

Note that we intentionally avoid using the term "worship leader" to dispel the misconception that only the music portion of the service is worship and encourage thinking of the entire experience as worship.

Producer

The producer is the most important role in worship development that many teams don't have. The person fulfilling this role is an overseer—the guardian of the theme. He or she is the project manager. It's worth mentioning again here that no one, including the producer, is to act as a gatekeeper for ideas. The producer is the point person and is to provide leadership in every area of worship development, from music to media to preaching, to ensure that the main idea of the service is present and that the various elements fit together into one seamless experience. This may happen in the meeting, but typically happens more so outside the design meeting. In our experience, the producer (as opposed to the preacher or some other party) often manages teams that function well. It is important that this function is truly about management, not micromanagement. Nothing kills the spirit of the team more than overmanaging every detail of the process.

Outside of the meeting, the producer empowers, equips, and coordinates the various staff and volunteer groups who have a hand in implementing the team's design. He or she may also act as the director of what can be a chaotic scene on the day of worship and manages a variety of tasks, from directing the technical rehearsal to touching base with media, altar, music, drama, and other groups to helping take care of last-minute details.

To be the leader of the team is not to be the creative decision maker. Although in some situations creative direction is a necessary part of the role's leadership, it is not the job of the producer to advance a personal creative agenda but rather to lead implementation of what the team decided as a group.

Some larger churches have a staff person with the title of "Creative Director," "Worship Arts Pastor," or the like. The person with this title is organizationally an ideal choice for the producer role. Traci Henegar is Worship Coordinator on the Trietsch team. She defines her role as "keeper of all details regarding Sunday services, arranger and procurer of elements needed for said services, and timekeeper extraordinaire on Sunday." The last part is crucial, as Trietsch juggles three services in a four-hour window every Sunday morning.

The producer is the most important role in worship development that the typical congregation probably doesn't have in place. She or he can be gifted in people skills or technical skills or both: so long as the individual is a leader. Consider some of the many functions of a producer:

- Write scripts for worship orders. Make sure everyone involved has one.
- Work with various teams and individuals throughout the week to empower and equip them in their respective ministry service areas.
- Coordinate with technical and creative teams for all details—from stage props to who gets which microphone.
- Develop and use a checklist of all standard tasks in preparing for worship. This is especially helpful should the church have to rely on a back-up producer.
- Make final preparations on the day of worship:
  ○ Start long before worship begins. Depending on the complexity of the experience, this could mean two or more hours.
  ○ Check all graphics, including song lyrics (preferably as the band rehearses them).
  ○ Run over sermon with preacher for graphic cues.
  ○ Confirm arrangement of altar displays and rehearse any scripts and spoken word segments with "the talent."
  ○ Check in with sound and lighting people to confirm cues and needs.
  ○ Carefully plan and rehearse transitions, with music, graphics, and animation.
  ○ Run a complete rehearsal, from beginning to end. Include everyone, with band, hosts, and so on; even the pastor, if possible.

(This is not just about checking microphone levels. It is important for people to get a feel for the service and transitions, and for the producer to see how all the pieces fit together.)
○ Repeat technical part as necessary, or portions of it.

During worship:
- Help people with cues and scripts, including the talent and technical types. Give cues for stage movement as necessary.
- Keep the experience moving like cruise control. Avoid down times and unintentional silence.
- Nudge people when it is time for them to move to the stage or the chancel.
- Take notes on good things and things to improve.
- Have extra candles, lighters, paper, pens, water bottles, and mints in a box for use during worship.

After worship:
- If producing multiple services, check in with everyone to confirm needs are met.
- Schedule brief between-service debriefings with the worship design team, if possible, to confirm what works or doesn't work, and make appropriate changes.
- Check new batteries, state of candles, and other items used during worship.

Writer

Themes, metaphors, and other techniques used to integrate the various elements of worship don't just emerge on their own. They must be intentionally cultivated prior to the live worship setting to make sure they are clear and understood to the congregation. This is where a writer comes in.

Some churches avoid reading prewritten words. If you're a part of such a congregation, having a writer doesn't mean changing your style. Many churches use a writer to create "talking points" and then allow the speaker to improvise while at the same time hitting on the key words that keep a worship service cohesive.

Writers pen specific language that helps bridge metaphors to ideas and makes themes evident. These connections can occur in a call to worship time, within musical sets, during prayer, as a part of a sermon, in drama, and in a variety of other ways. During these times, have specific language prepared for the speaker to use.

Consider, for example, what is called the "theme setup." What is a theme setup? you ask. The theme setup is a sort of creative call to worship in which the worship host connects the worshiper with the theme or metaphor for the weekend. What is a worship host? you ask. A worship host is a primary up-front person besides the pastor. His or her job is to offer spoken words during the service, such as the call to worship, prayer, welcome, and announcements. In some churches the bandleader performs this function, but having a separate worship host is recommended. In more traditional settings, this person might be referred to as the liturgist. As the writer of the Trietsch team, Len composes the theme setup for each week of worship, which he either delivers himself in worship or hands off to the worship host. Every host at Len's church knows that he or she can take the words as is or modify them and personalize them as needed to help make his or her delivery more natural.

There is a certain formula to the theme setup. It begins with the connectional element. Sometimes this is a response to a video and sometimes it is a "have you ever" question or a statement of life experience. It is often humorous. For a weekend theme using coffee filters as modern-day examples of purity and separating wheat from chaff, the theme setup followed an explanatory coffeehouse video with the question, "Do you remember your favorite cup of coffee, ever?" A weekend on stewardship in troubled economic times included a scene from the film *Fun with Dick and Jane* (where an out-of-work Dick piles a foot-high salad on one plate at the $2.99 buffet) followed by a theme setup talking about dealing with financial adversity.

The second element ties in the scriptural and thematic overview. In the aforementioned coffee service, the connectional questions about good and bad coffee experiences was followed by an explanation of purity as found in Luke 3:15-17. The stewardship example, which was based on the human condition of fear, followed the film clip and made the connection with "perfect love drives out fear." A good theme setup script makes sure to tie in the title of the service. For coffee, that meant closing with the line "Let's live pure to the last drop" as a main image on the screen showing the same title appeared.

It is not necessary for the worship host to be part of the design team, as the writer will formulate scripts based on the design team's creativity. The host may be considered a part of one of many extensions of the creative team, just as there are musicians who are a part of worship but who don't design worship.

Technical director

The technical director is the team's representative for all things media, including sound, lighting, projection, and stage. Because of the technical challenges often associated with planning big ideas on short notice, this person is frequently under much job performance pressure. This can cause some grumpiness in the team meeting, and may also result in taking creative shortcuts. The disgruntled tech director might look for ways to not accomplish the big ideas that are generated if he or she is approaching burnout. Good communication and plenty of lead time on major changes will ease the pressure and frustration felt by the tech director.

In our experience the technical director often has a tendency to see himself or herself as a gatekeeper of others' ideas. We sometimes joke at seminars that the technical director, for some reason, is often grumpy. The reason for this may have something to do with a sense of being undervalued and underappreciated in what is essentially a support role. In such a light it is natural to want to underpromise and overdeliver, or to say something cannot be done and then quietly set about trying to accomplish the requested task. The challenge for the technical director is to stay upbeat and supportive, while the challenge for the team is to recognize the challenges of the job and provide much support and encouragement.

Creative people

A good team also has a number of people with specific creative skills. These can range from video production to graphic arts, drama, and much more. One team had someone whose creative skill was an incredible knowledge of movies. For any topic, this member could name two or three great movie clips.

On the Trietsch team, Len serves in the role of creative director and leads the creative discussion, which includes both creative suggestions and ideas, and a lot of directed questions, such as "What is the goal of the service?" or "What are we doing here exactly?"

This is not to say that Len corners the market, because everyone in the room is creative. Everyone in the room engages in the conversation, and there are a number of people whose primary role is creative. The director of media, Alan Miles, describes his role on the team as both creative and organizational: "I am responsible for video segment ideas and implementation, as well as helping in the creative process as far as theme and metaphor, along with graphics. I am also responsible for communicating to the weekend media teams what is to happen on Sunday morning." Paul Bonneau serves as a member of the music staff: "I contribute ideas and respond to ideas in the initial brainstorming process. I give my opinions on the pertinence and relevancy of ideas as I see them as being applicable to current trends and motions in our immediate culture and society. I bring specific suggestions regarding music programming in worship services." Frank Hames, the church's pianist, says he is there for "creative input and comic relief." (Too bad his jokes aren't funnier! Just kidding, Frank.)

The specific creative talents on your team will be unique and a reflection of your church community. Learn not to worry about talents unavailable to your team and instead to focus on improving the skills that are available.

New believer

A role that many teams never consider is that of a new believer. Even without knowing it, many worship planners and pastors infuse a churchy or "Christianese" language into the written, spoken, and visual word. This creates a problem for unchurched or slightly churched visitors who are not well versed in this strange tongue.

One visitor remarked that she thought church was going to end with a card game after hearing the pastor say that they would partake in Holy Eucharist later in the service. This of course means Communion to those of us who know the language, but for someone new to the faith, it can be a confusing concept.

New believers help worship designers put the message into layperson's terms. They can help flesh out hard-to-grasp concepts and they can bring new perspectives that make the message stronger. If there are terms used in the design meeting that don't make sense to the outsider, the new believer can help identify them to be changed, or at the very least to be explained in a new way.

Other roles may play an important part in the team meeting or may come into play outside the planning session, including a scribe (someone gifted at writing down all of the team's ideas and disseminating them to everyone later) and a display guru (someone who creates altar displays each week that reflect the day's theme and metaphor).

To Do

Get together with your team and think about the following questions. Try to encourage honest and open participation.

- Which role or roles resonate with each member of your team? Discuss, allowing everyone in the room an opportunity to share.
- Are there any additional roles not described here that apply to your team? Name them and share a vision for what the role is.
- Who—if anyone—on the team does not feel that she or he has a role to play?

CHAPTER EIGHT

HOW DO WE
ORGANIZE OUR TIME?

Whether you are in a small or large church, with a brand-new or a well-established worship team, finding a schedule that team members can agree on and commit to is a significant challenge. Small churches, with limited staff and time, may have obvious road-blocks. Even larger or staff-heavy churches often feel they cannot devote a number of full-time employees to the worship design process. Don't let this become an excuse that prevents you from exploring the power of team-based worship planning. The good news is that all of these things can be overcome.

Many all-volunteer teams excel in planning creative, engaging worship. In a smaller church, volunteers are the only option. In a larger church, your staff might have to think like volunteers. Consider an amateur softball league. Many people give up a night every week to play nine innings of ball. Some even find time to have weekly practices in addition to games. Dedicated volunteer worship teams, when given the opportunity to play and succeed, will quickly find time for their own "love of the game" and the effect it has on God's kingdom.

Many churches already conduct a regular worship planning time. In a large church, it is often a gathering of pastors, musicians, and tech people—everyone who is involved in worship. In a small church, it is frequently the pastor and the music leader exchanging emails or standing in the hallway together for a few minutes. Ideally, however, a weekly worship design team meeting should be more than a calendar-sharing session. You are designing a worship event where lives are transformed through the creative presentation of the Gospel. Each worship element is not pre-determined but should be developed together as a group.

Frequency: How Often to Meet

The first factor to determine is how often the team will meet. While worship styles vary wildly across regions, denominations, and congregational sizes, there seem to be only a few basic models for planning. We've outlined three popular methods below with some notes. This is not meant to be a comprehensive list but rather a starting point for figuring out your church's own unique solution.

Single team meeting weekly

This is perhaps the most common model for designing worship in a team. A weekly worship team can be staff, volunteer, or a mix of the two. There is a set weekly time, either during the workday or in the evening. It is recommended that this design team time and day remain generally the same each week. For example, Tuesdays at 2:00 p.m. might work well with an all-staff team. Evenings will probably be better if volunteers are involved.

In some ways, the weekly meeting is an easier model, particularly in terms of facilitating the logistics of planning. Small church planning structures, which are often highly relationship-driven, rely on ongoing communication between the preacher, music leader, and other staff or volunteer team members. This communication happens face to face during the meeting but also, and sometimes to a greater degree, takes place outside the team meeting via email and telephone.

Weekly meetings are also—arguably—easier in terms of managing interpersonal dynamics, because the team members have more interaction with each other. This presumably leads to stronger relationships. (Of course, a high level of team interaction can have the opposite effect, but in our experience the more often a team meets the better its members form and maintain relationships.) If team members have sufficiently flexible schedules to do weekly meetings, the overall closeness of the team will likely be much stronger just because of the frequency of the gatherings.

More likely than not, teams that meet weekly are going to be staff. Understand that for many staff members, the idea of "another meeting" isn't something that will be relished at first. Be proactive about making the meetings uplifting, casual, creative, and fun. If done right, "design team day" will become the highlight of the week.

Multiple teams meeting weekly or on rotation

Although weekly worship planning has its pros, one of its cons is that it can become exhausting, especially for volunteers who have busy lives outside of the team. Burnout can happen pretty fast. Having multiple teams sharing the worship design burden can be a great solution to this problem.

In this model, several different teams design worship. For example, there may be four teams, each meeting once a month with the paid staff (usually a pastor, a music person, and a media specialist). The paid staff come to every meeting and help carry out the individual services. Planning could be for the upcoming week, or it may be for several weeks ahead.

Usually this method of planning includes a mix of preacher, music leader, and key technical and creative volunteers. It might also be made up of an all-staff team. The worship producer is the link and becomes highly important to keeping continuity between teams., Teams that don't have a producer in place should add one before moving forward on this method.

The length of these meetings can vary, but ideally they are around two to three hours. It is not necessary to determine every single song, prayer, and creative element within the group meeting time, but deciding the overall creative (theme/metaphor) direction for the service, and an order of worship should be the goal. Individuals outside the meeting can then carry out specific tasks.

Churches who preach in series, use the Revised Common Lectionary, or follow a standard liturgy may find this method particularly useful, since the structure of the church calendar can facilitate planning ahead. However, such a structure is dependent on a preacher who plans ahead.

Single team meeting once every few weeks or monthly

If filling one good team—much less a whole bunch of them—seems like an enormous task, consider using one team but spreading the meetings out to once or twice a month. This third common model may be the most realistic model for small and mostly volunteer-based teams.

The overarching goal in this model is to set the creative direction for several services at one meeting. When teams come together, the view is like a lens kept on wide-angle. Meetings are for brainstorming themes, metaphors, songs, and other creative elements for upcoming services. Only devote an hour or so to each service, hopefully less. Using this model means that more creative decisions are made outside of the meetings by individuals communicating via email, text, and telephone.

As you put your team together or restructure your existing team, keep in mind the things that can deflate the team. One detractor to morale often comes from looking at the way other "successful" teams prepare. At most large church conferences, the official playbook reads: (a) worship is the primary event of the congregation, so (b) it is due the most resources, and (c) if given adequate resources, it will produce a growing church. In other words, act like a big church in the approach to worship design, and eventually you'll become a big church. This may or may not be true. Examples may be cited either way. Even if it is true, however, not every congregation seeks to become a clone of its most frequently modeled mega-church. Enjoy the freedom you have to discover your own indigenous structure for designing worship!

Agenda: How to Meet

Let's be realistic: "Agenda" is not a very popular word with creative people. It usually ranks somewhere near the bottom of the list between "taxes" and "sunrise." The word itself belies its intent. An agenda is simply a guide for how to meet. To make the most of our time, we need to establish a regular process for our team meetings. Successful sports teams don't begin practice without a game plan in mind, and you shouldn't either. As with frequency, various solutions exist according to the gifts and the needs of each individual team. Here's one sample model for your worship design team:

Small group development/prayer (10-45 minutes)

Focus your initial attention on nurturing and developing Christian community within your worship design teams. The sense of "safe space" and "what is said here, stays here" is crucial to fostering creativity and modeling life as the body of Christ to the congregation.

If the meeting is held during a workday, this time may be limited to ten to fifteen minutes, with mutual sharing and prayer. If meeting in the evening, the team may consider a longer "small group" time prior to worship planning. The less frequently the team sees one another outside of the meeting, the more critical this step is.

We have worked on some teams that took small group development seriously. Others assumed that because they met regularly and were all Christians, they'd automatically take on the nature of a small group. This is not necessarily the case.

One team Len worked with only met once a month. Since the team took the small group covenant seriously, they would spend forty-five minutes to an hour over dinner, sharing personal life stories and struggles and prayer, before ever moving to the work of worship.

Debrief time (10-15 minutes)

Taking a few minutes to evaluate what happened in the previous week's worship can be very instructive. This may entail comments from each team member regarding successes and failures or specific feedback they have heard from an attendee. It may also be a focused discussion on ways to improve a single aspect of the worship process.

Len worked with one church that had a tendency to drift toward discussions of problems with sound during this period of the meeting. Every week's meeting ended up as a "gripe session" over such topics as dropped wireless microphones or missed cues, in spite of the fact that the team agreed such discussions weren't very helpful. The team finally solved their "sound problem" by buying an egg timer. Each week in the meeting, when the debrief stage began, a team member would pull out the egg timer and set it to 10 minutes. When the buzzer sounded, all debriefing, including the weekly sound discussion, was done.

Word (10-20 minutes)

With debriefing done, the preacher lays out the basis for the upcoming worship experience.

A warning: this is a difficult art to master. We have seen many preachers, used to operating as lone rangers, develop too much while getting used to the team process. Let's create a sample preacher called Rev. I. M. Dunn, who comes to the meeting with core and supplemental scripture texts, main points, and illustrations already noted. Pastor Dunn has the notes pre-written and has already passed them out as a Word document outline via email, supposedly to foster creative thinking. Or even worse, the team receives the notes orally in detailed fashion, in a way that doesn't foster openness and discussion.

Occasionally, Rev. Dunn's method works. When creative people look over the pastor's notes and come prepared with notes about themes, titles, metaphors, and creative elements, it can jumpstart an open discussion. In our experience, however, this is rare. More often, the result is squelched creativity. People often treat the notes as a final copy rather than a draft and are unable or unwilling to offer or accept changes or modifications.

Even in the media age, there is still much power in the printed word to create a sense of finality.

Rev. Dunn's model is only likely to work on a veteran team operating with a high degree of mutual experience and trust. Even then it can undermine creative potential.

Others, wanting to utilize the creativity of the team, bring too little. In this scenario, the preacher (let's call this one Rev. I. Dunno) comes to the meeting with, well, nothing, save a general hunch about a direction and maybe some potential texts that match the season, series, or Christian calendar. Rev. Dunno understands the power of the creative team, but he provides insufficient direction on which the team can brainstorm. The result is often brainstorms that are only "brain mists," or even "brainsunshinydays." There is little creative traction, and the team suffers through long periods of awkward silence.

Both Dunn and Dunno miss the potential of the team. Good team worship design happens under the thoughtful direction of a preacher who is capable of providing a core scripture, general reflections, and even a personal illustration or two. This preacher, though, knows how and when to open up discussion, talking a little but not too much, and then asking questions to elicit helpful feedback.

Brainstorm (30-60 minutes)

The previous stage, Word, and this stage blend together on good teams. For example, as the preacher shares reflections on a scripture or a story, someone in the room makes a mental jump—"oh, that reminds me of a movie I saw recently!" Pastoral, theological, cultural, visual, artistic, and technological discussions intermingle during this time, which is the most exciting part of the process and the reason most people sign on.

This time may last up to an hour or more. There might be periods of silence and periods in which everyone has something to share and is equally passionate. Creativity can be both quiet and fierce. Do not fear this process. Embrace it, and let it run free. The more openly the team allows itself to think, the better worship will be.

Brainstorming is so vital, chapter 12 is devoted entirely to the process.

Decision (10-20 minutes)

Brainstorming eventually reaches a point of diminishing returns. This point is usually obvious; it is when a series of good ideas begins to be followed by much worse ideas. When this happens, it's time to look for con-sensus on the main idea of the service and its theme, metaphor, and goals.

On the main idea, consensus is vital. Does everyone in the room agree on what the upcoming worship service is about? Can the theme be artic-ulated in a sentence or two? What is the primary means to communicate the theme? What is the primary visual metaphor? The title? Is there a col-lective goal for the service, such as an offer of salvation or a call to action on a specific mission project? The more the team can agree on these details, the clearer the service will be. A tiny degree of confusion at this point can blossom into full chaos later, so be careful.

The decision stage may or may not include a specific order of worship (see Frequency, above). Teams that cannot make time for decisions within the meeting time can charge a member with this task for later dis-tribution via email.

Lather, rinse, repeat (optional)

Some teams have the set goal of designing multiple services in one meeting. For these teams, the next step is to start over at the "Word" stage with a different text, hopefully following a break.

Administrative (10 minutes)

Place all housekeeping tasks at the end of the meeting when everyone is ready to go. This ensures that they don't take over valuable planning time.

Being intentional about how often you meet and how you meet can make all of the difference in how your team's "season" ends. If you want your team to experience more wins than losses, take the time to figure out when and how you should prepare for the big game. Remember, team development is a process, and the most important thing is how those in worship see Jesus through our performance during "the big game."

PART THREE

TAKING FLIGHT

Achieving Koinonia

*Many teams form, but many fail. What separates
those that take flight is an elusive quality called
koinonia, the transformative synergy of Holy Spirit-
driven team collaboration that would be impossible if
attempted by any one person. Koinonia is the purpose
of having teams in the first place—the experience of
being a part of something great. Koinonia is truly
living as the body of Christ.*

BECOMING A SMALL GROUP

Three days before the first successful flight, Wilbur Wright climbed aboard the Flyer and began the sixty-foot journey down the monorail runway the two brothers had constructed for takeoff, hoping to make history. That attempt, their first, ended in a dramatic crash that damaged several components of the plane. Instead of disappointment, the brothers felt hope. In that aborted takeoff they discovered that their aeroplane could actually fly, as the nose had lifted off the ground momentarily before coming back to earth.

Although thankfully not all team experiences begin with such harrowing crashes, it is important to understand that creativity can be dangerous and may inflict potentially harmful wounds on its participants—if not physical, then certainly emotional and even spiritual.

Being creative in a group can feel a lot like barreling down a makeshift runway toward an uncertain outcome. First of all, participating in the creative process can be somewhat risky for one's ego. To be creative means opening oneself to rejection, and for most of us, experiencing rejection hurts. It's probably why most of us are prone to beginning an idea pitch with qualifying statements such as, "This may be a bad idea, but..." and other words that will make the crash less painful if our brainstorms are not well received.

As any right-brained person can testify, it is difficult not to get ego and identity tied up in one's ideas and work. Whereas developing a thick skin can be helpful in combating the fear that comes from rejected ideas, it's easier said than done. Much can be said about not taking negative critical feedback personally, but most creative people are very sensitive to how others perceive them. Insecurities can cause good worship designers to remain grounded, so it's an imperative to create an environment that fosters the creative process.

Safe Space

It is important when working with others to create what many teams we've been on have labeled "safe space." Safe space is crucial—maybe the single most important element in the worship design process. If you take only one idea from reading this book, it would be this: create safe space for the team to operate!

Safe space is achieved when everyone in the room feels that they are free to be themselves without being judged for what's going on in and outside of the room. We define safe space as a place of confidentiality, professionalism, and lack of judgment. It is the redeemed, worship design equivalent of the Las Vegas slogan "What happens here stays here."

Safe space is separate from the general issue of trust, or even of friendship. Not everyone in the room is best friends or would go out together for dinner. But they do offer one another professional acceptance and are willing to judge the merits of an idea rather than the individual expressing them. Safe space is a requirement for the open exchange of ideas to flow freely. In every design team that we have either participated in or observed there has been a direct correlation between the ability of the team to unleash powerful, creative worship and the ability of that team to trust one another.

Creative people must have safe space. Paul Bonneau, a music professional on the Trietsch team, appreciates the team's ability to operate in safe space. He says, "What is very effective about our team is that we are all able to leave ego out of the equation when bringing forth ideas and incorporating or rejecting ideas. It is a very safe place to disagree vehemently on ideas considered." Without the safety of knowing that what is said in the room will stay there, the honest exchange of ideas is muted.

Safe space doesn't just magically appear on its own. It is the result of much hard work—just like any successful interpersonal relationship.

One large United Methodist church in Texas, averaging more than three thousand in worship every weekend, tried worship design teams for a while but gave up. As described to Len, the senior pastor had a hard time opening up creatively to his staff team. He simply didn't trust them. That is not to say there are people on the team he mistrusted; he may have trusted every person in the room at least on some level. He may have not trusted the process or the entity that was the collection of people together. Now this church just designs worship around the ideas of the two lead pastors. The pastor duo make regular road trips in the senior pastor's convertible, exchanging ideas. The creativity generated from the two is then passed along to other groups, around which the services are built.

Cognizant or not, that senior pastor didn't feel safe space within the aborted team effort, but does feel it with his fellow pastor on staff. This two-person process may work on occasion for the church. But imagine if, instead of the power of two, the church was able to tap into the power of the entire group, not once the direction is set, but at the idea formation stage. We believe if they could somehow form an atmosphere around worship design where everyone feels that he or she is in safe space that the impact of the team would increase greatly.

That senior pastor may have discovered that real brainstorming is messy, and often there are creative dry spells where it seems the only ideas being offered are bad ideas. The longer the room is silent, the harder it can become to generate ideas. Insecurity can begin to drive the creative process. Safe space helps tremendously in these times because team members feel the freedom to suggest ideas ranging from the absurd to the possibly brilliant, knowing that they won't be ridiculed or judged by whatever ideas they offer. In a safe environment, it is even possible to mutually laugh at the creative struggle.

The importance of safe space should not be underestimated when it comes to brainstorming. Without even realizing it, individuals can become a hindrance to the creative process just by the approach they take. Overeager creative types might monopolize the discussion. Maybe you've witnessed these personalities:

- "Creative bullies" (yes, they exist) spend more time making fun of or shooting down ideas teammates present than in offering their own good ideas.
- "Overqualifiers" spend as much time setting up why their idea might not work or how it might be a bad idea as they do in actually pitching the idea.
- "Justifiers" use a passive-aggressive approach in constantly stating why their idea is still worth considering long after consensus is reached and the team has moved on.

Establishing a Small Group

Separate from safe space is the power of the team that is unleashed when the team becomes a small group. Whereas safe space may be found in professional and secular environments, according to our definition, a small group is uniquely Christian.

Many churches separate spiritual and developmental functions in daily organizational life. To suggest that a planning team operate as a small group, emphasizing mutual trust, spiritual formation, and accountability, may seem counterintuitive. But in the course of worship design, we have repeatedly seen it is necessary and a clear indicator of the power of the group to facilitate worship.

There are many resources devoted to small group ministry. For the purposes of worship design, we are applying three definitions to a worship design team small group, in sequential order.

Camaraderie

First is the ability of the team to have fun together. Does the team laugh, have fun, and enjoy one another's company? Friendship in the name of ministry is powerful and the basis for every other aspect of the small group experience.

Some teams we know have gone so far as to schedule activities to increase camaraderie, such as laser tag or bowling. If doing these, just watch out for those creative bullies!

Mutual trust

Mutual trust is the second step. If you're in a team now, does your team have it? Professional safe space begins to grow into a true small group when mutual trust is fostered, usually by the activities of spiritual formation. As worship designers, we must be about more than just the task of filling out an order of worship. Becoming a small group means finding deep points of connection through prayer, study, and directed fellowship. By directed, we mean that simply chatting isn't enough. A small group atmosphere must be fostered. The result is truly transformational worship that is designed and created in the presence of the Holy Spirit.

In our experience, a good venue for creating a true small group often involves combining our meeting time with a meal of some sort. At the breaking of bread together, worship design task conversation is off-limits. The purpose of the meal is to share the team's highs and lows, to talk about what's going on in personal lives, and to continue to build community. A small group atmosphere doesn't just happen; a team has to be intentional about building it. Aside from choosing the right people to be on the team, this may be the most important aspect of team development and formation.

Recently we did a workshop in a small hotel conference room. The size of the room and number of participants allowed much more back-and-forth interaction than we would have from the stage during a typical seminar. Throughout our session on teams, there was one gentleman squirming and occasionally asking a question. He seemed to be struggling to put his finger on exactly what was keeping his team on the ground. After nearly an hour of hearing much of what you're reading in this book, he stood up and said, "I don't get it! Our team fits every characteristic you've listed here in this workshop and we just don't seem to be able to achieve success."

We went through our checklist point by point and compared our principles to his team. He proudly checked off each item. Then we asked, "Is your team functioning as a small group?" His face and posturing told the rest of the story. He said, "Well, no, not really. We're all staff and we're so busy, we don't really have time for that." That was all we needed to hear.

Having everything you'd ever need—from the right skills represented, the right people in place, a comfortable meeting room, a sufficient budget, to a willing pastor—cannot make up for the lack of koinonia in the room. It has to be nurtured, and that starts with mutual trust.

As your team is being formed (or reformed), build into the development a time to assess the group's trust level. In some teams, talking about it will not work, because the attitude of the team does not provide the safety needed to speak openly. In this case, have team members submit their thoughts anonymously and work through them together as a group.

Here are a few sample questions to consider:

1. Do you feel free to share ideas in this group?
2. If not, what would you say prevents you from feeling the freedom to share?
3. What are we doing well in creating a safe creative environment?
4. What are we doing that detracts from creative space?

Creating mutual trust as the basis for a small group is even more important when working with mostly volunteers. The majority of churches we encounter design worship with one or two paid staff and several volunteers. The lack of regular face time that typically occurs for all or mostly staff teams can become an obstacle when working with all or mostly volunteer teams. It is important to build extra small group time in when working with unpaid worship designers so that relationships can be strengthened and comfort levels broadened.

Spiritual formation and accountability

Ultimately, a true small group functions to disciple its members. Even though this is a group designed around the specific task of designing worship, discipleship functions may occur if given the opportunity.

For example, more than a one-time exercise, make a discussion like the one on evaluating trust levels part of an ongoing window of small group development. Maybe consider devoting ten to fifteen minutes to small group time at the onset of each meeting. This is apropos if your church is small and your team is entirely volunteer or if your church is large and your team entirely staff. Eat dinner together. Pray together. Find ways to grow the spiritual intimacy of the group. Kris Melvin, worship leader on the Trietsch team, rightly states that a team that works on its relationship with God together grows closer and gains more trust together and ultimately improves worship: "If we can learn to fully trust each other and grow closer to God together, our team could really feed off each other. I can only imagine what God could do in the services when we plan from God and not our own ideas."

Out of the deep relationships of Christlike intimacy, amazing creative things can happen.

Keeping the group together

When things really start to work, when the team begins spending as much time in the air as on the ground and the congregation grows to expect powerful weekly worship, success may quickly lead to burnout. If teams don't work to keep the process fresh, what was once exhilarating and full of wonder in time can become the weekly drudge.

Say your team is composed of six people. Three of those people are good friends outside of the team; they hang out, go to movies together, and even maybe holiday together with their families. It is our experience that just because half of the team is buddies there is no assurance that the team will have the same level of closeness. That small group is an interpersonal relationship times six. It has its own identity and must form its own relationship, starting from the first time the team comes together.

At our first local church, the two of us made up half of the four-person creative worship design team. We moved to a new ministry and again made up half of that team. Our thinking at the time was, *This will be easy. We already know the process, so we'll be able to help the others along and pick right up where we left off!* That was not the case. In fact, we did end up creating powerful worship together, but it was only after starting completely over and learning how to design worship as a new group of four.

The same thing happened again to Jason. After Lumicon, Jason joined the worship team at a church plant. This group had two other members with experience on a successful worship design team. Once again, as we had previously discovered, in spite of the experience level of the team's individual members, instead of diving right into the deep end, the team had to go through the slow process of wading through the shallow water of trust development.

If it is necessary to change the composition of the team's members, realize that you are going to start over at square one when it comes to trust.

Worship teams are like software. Each time you introduce a new person to the team it is like releasing an entirely new version where the code has been rewritten from scratch. If the old team was version 1.0, the addition of a new member doesn't make the team version 1.1; it makes the team version 2.0, because the new person in the room has relationships, or the lack of a relationship, with every other person in the room. So back to square one on trust development!

Because each team has its own group identity aside from the relationships of its members, it is important that the team's members not come and go. There's a word for that sort of group: a committee. Committees are all about the task. Worship design teams that work are about more than the task. In this environment, worship becomes a sacred reflection of the relationships formed within the team. It is the body of Christ, designing and living together, out of which God is glorified.

The difference between the organic, living team and the cold, task team is obvious. Which is yours?

Avoid the Trap of the Work of Worship

The Wright Flyer wasn't the only plane that the brothers built. They kept breaking new ground as time went on. Successful teams must strive to do the same. If worship planners don't continue to innovate and focus on the real reasons for designing worship in the first place, it won't be long before the regular design team meetings are only about the work of worship design.

Being focused solely on the work of worship design means coming into the room and wanting to just get through all of the particulars as fast as possible. When the focus centers on how fast this can be done, much is compromised, and worship might as well be planned using a Magic 8 ball.

One particularly hard week, a worship design team was struggling to get all of the components of worship working in a cohesive way. After several stalls, someone in the room said, "We need to get this thing 100 percent of the way there." The pastor responded with the words, "Eighty percent is good enough this week." His statement was both disheartening and scary. The week that 80 percent is enough may be the week that an unchurched member of the community curiously walks in to worship wondering if there is something there for them. Thank God Jesus didn't think 80 percent was good enough!

The reality of worship design is that the harder we work to convey the message in creative ways, the easier we make it for our congregations to receive it. The weeks that the attitude is "Let's just make this a simple one" are the weeks our congregations are forced to work harder to understand the message.

It is of the utmost importance to remember that what we do in worship design team meetings is possibly the most important thing we'll ever do in life. We are telling the most important story there is to tell, and if our hearts aren't in it or we just want to get it over with we are taking a serious risk with the lives of those who will enter our sanctuaries. If we succeed in crafting services that are creative, engaging, and full of the Holy Spirit, we will see lives transformed. Like the Flyer lifting off to soar in the air for the first time, the hearts of individuals might finally know the gospel in a way that is authentic, powerful, and real to the world that we live in today.

The key to avoiding the "work of worship" mind-set is bathing the process in prayer and study. If we are ever to redeem cultural metaphors and stories, we have to dig deep into Scripture and be guided by the Holy Spirit in our worship production. In our experience, there is a direct relationship between how well the creativity flows and how much prayer is involved in the process.

We were part of two very successful worship design teams that had drastically different approaches to the process. One of the two teams (we'll call them Team A—how creative of us) was made up of people with mind-sets about as varied as could be. Age differences, political backgrounds, and other work-related tensions made this group more challenging outside of the meetings. The second of the two teams (we'll call them, yes, Team B) had very like-minded individuals on it. Outside the team meeting we often spent time together socializing, going to dinner, and just enjoying one another's company.

Team A would gather (many times directly after dealing with other work-related tension) and would start with an extended time of prayer and study; sometimes this would last twenty minutes or more. However, Team B would gather to design worship and would jump pretty quickly into the meat for the service being designed. It was rare that we ever started first with prayer or directed biblical study. The pastor in Team B would go so far as to say, "I was up at 5:30 this morning in personal devotional time. We're all prayed up."

Yet, somehow all of the work tensions of Team A would melt away and in the time that Team B could spend creating one service, Team A would regularly design three or more services. This is in direct contrast to the closeness or camaraderie associated with the teams.

Although both models were successful, we attribute the power of prayer and study to the speed, depth, and accomplishments found in the first team. It wasn't that Team B wasn't praying for worship design; it was that prayer was often happening outside the meeting as individuals. Worship design should be bathed in group prayer, with *group* being the key word.

Upon reflecting on the two teams' approaches, we began to think more about Matthew 18:20: "For where two or three come together in my name, there am I with them." To really take flight, worship designers must pray together.

On the day that humankind was no longer bound to the ground, a team of two brothers and five lifeguards hauled a six-hundred-pound "flying machine" to the top of a hill to make history. This small group achieved something that forever changed the world in which we live. Wilbur and Orville never could have managed to get that plane off the ground if it weren't for the others who helped them carry the burden. In the same way, worship planning has the ability to soar to new heights when we gather as small groups in God's name to achieve God's mission on Earth.

LEARNING TO MAKE DECISIONS TOGETHER

I f you design worship as a team, take this little quiz.

1. My favorite worship planning sessions are when:
   (a) We find a creative idea that everyone gets excited about
   (b) Everyone listens to my ideas, since my ideas are best
   (c) Nobody gets injured

2. When participating in a worship team design meeting:
   (a) Everyone engages in a group dialogue, sharing ideas in an orderly fashion
   (b) Everyone gets excited and speaks at once
   (c) Getting people to share requires low-level torture techniques

3. When listening to my teammate share a concept:
   (a) I am eager to share more creative ideas
   (b) I think up witty replies to show how stupid the idea is
   (c) I patiently wait for that person to shut up so I can talk

4. My worship design team:
   (a) Has experienced conflict
   (b) Is currently experiencing conflict
   (c) Will experience conflict

5. After the meeting:
   (a) I am proud of the service we as a team have created
   (b) I would prefer that others not know I was involved
   (c) I anticipate telling the whole church about all of *my* great ideas

There are some goofy answers in this quiz, to be sure, but it gets at the heart of the decision-making process. This is the goal for any team, whether planning worship or any other endeavor: to engage in a group decision-making process. Those who put together a team, at a basic level, believe that there is potentially greater value in the decision-making power of a group of like-minded and passionate people than in a single person acting alone.

Yet, ironically, one of the biggest obstacles to good teamwork is learning to make decisions together. Is it possible for creative, sometimes headstrong individuals to collaborate in a way about which everyone feels good?

We believe strongly that it is. Unfortunately, knowing team worship design is possible—and potentially powerful—and getting there are two very different things. One of the most pragmatic and challenging aspects of team dynamics is the process of learning to make decisions together.

The Broken Body

In far too many churches for far too long, worship has been planned in a segregated, somewhat egocentric way. The leader of each aspect of worship works in his or her office alone, preparing his or her part of worship in isolation. Unfortunately, this is often done with little to no consideration of how it will fit with the other aspects of worship, which are also being prepared with the same disregard for cohesiveness.

Is this how we are called to carry out our ministry here on Earth? We are called to be the body of Christ, yet we design worship as if we are prosthetic limbs that can be attached and detached at will. By breaking the body into pieces throughout the week (in preparation for the weekend) we limit the potential power of what worship could be.

In an attempt to get past this broken body, many churches form teams for the purpose of designing a more cohesive worship experience. The problem is that this move toward group design often comes without a change in mentality. Even if planning is now occurring in the same physical space, individuals come to team meetings with the same isolated thinking about their respective area(s) of responsibility.

Maybe you've experienced a team meeting where each person in the room seems to be focused only on his or her own agenda. In these meetings, people aren't really listening as much as they are waiting for their own opportunity to speak. *Team* doesn't mean much if individuals can't move away from their individual agendas.

How a Team Makes Decisions

In this broken body out of which most of us come, our attitudes and agendas affect our decision-making ability. How are decisions reached in such an environment? In our experience, there are a variety of ways— some healthier than others—in which decisions are made as a team.

By single dominant individual
Teams in this situation serve little to no value. A single person, often the pastor but sometimes a producer or worship leader, dictates to the team theme(s), direction, creative elements, and even structure.

By minority
This is unfortunately a common problem with worship teams: a small group, either in the meeting itself or at another time and place, makes strategic decisions. Their expectation is that their decision is final, and the larger team merely exists to provide nonstrategic creative input or just to put a stamp of approval on what has been decided.

Although not as severe as a problem as number one, this also devalues and disrespects the team.

By majority
This is a team situation where more than half of those involved in the team make the decisions and where that decision is binding for all concerned.

It's possible this can become an effective model, but there is danger in excluding the opinions of diverse team members, as there can be great value in listening to all opinions. For example, a team consists almost entirely of twenty-somethings, except for a lone forty-something. The twenty-something members make stylistic decisions as a team, some of which the forty-something member doesn't like. The majority can discount the older member's input and go with what they personally prefer, or (hopefully) realize that the older member provides a valuable perspective for reaching and growing the congregation and make an active attempt to solicit the person's input.

By compromise

This happens when after exploring all options team members agree on an option they can all live with. The "live with" part is critical here. Say, for example, there is a disagreement about a visual interpretation of the concept of prayer. After some brainstorming there are three ideas on the board: fuel, telecommunications, and science. Part of the team likes the fuel angle (prayer as the petroleum that drives our spiritual engines). Part of the team likes the science angle (prayer as the "missing link" that solves the mystery of the gap between us and God). Since the team cannot agree between the two, everyone settles on a telecommunications angle (prayer as the wireless connection; "Can you hear me now?"). Compromise shouldn't be confused with consensus, which is both more effective and harder to achieve. "Settling" for an idea is not usually associated with being inspired by an idea. Great worship rarely follows compromises in worship planning.

Note that it isn't uncommon for those who have agreed in public to a particular course of action to quietly disagree behind closed doors, which can lead to division and strife in the team. That is why it's best to work through creative differences until consensus can be reached.

By consensus

Consensus is by far the best of the above options. A 100 percent commitment is needed for decisions of critical importance. Creative inspiration arises from a common conviction in the power of a particular idea. In consensus, each person fully agrees to the action to be taken, and everyone concerned fully subscribes to the decision made. It may require a great deal of information and time to reach consensus as a team, or it can happen almost instantly.

Which of these decision-making styles most closely resembles your current worship process? Take some time and reflect on the five options.

On Consensus

Although challenging, the ideal of any good worship design team is consensus on the service's theme and metaphor, directions and goals, creative elements, and structure.

Some don't believe in consensus, saying it is an idealized fantasy and too difficult to achieve in real-world situations. We think it is possible in real-world situations, but within a specific understanding of what the word *consensus* specifically means.

A post on the online blog "Journey to Authenticity" stated:

> I know the word compromise has its place but I deal with human relationships daily and I am finding the word consensus more respectful. I define consensus as a win-win versus compromise a lose-lose. Consensus thought is hard work and often unattainable because of our human constraints, i.e. pride, time, laziness, lack of commitment to one another, etc. Plus our culture is built around competition rather than team building. All this makes consensus building a foreign and counter-intuitive concept.
>
> I was explaining to someone that when you build consensus all parties involved "buy in" and it has to be done from genuine-ness and honesty. It requires people to say to themselves "I have my way of thinking about something but I could be wrong. So I am going to listen to you and allow my mind to be influenced by you. I may not fully agree but hopefully by sharing and listening we can agree to a new solution that is ours." The tough part is staying in the dialogue long enough to build that consensus and I believe that is where our impatience and laziness come into play. . . . As the group gets bigger the more likely compromise will need to have a place in the dialogue but even then the more points one can build consensus on the healthier the resolution will be.[1]

Consensus does not refer to complete and total agreement on personal preferences. Rather, consensus occurs when there is agreement that the message is good for the congregation—not that it's good for the personal preferences of the preacher, producer, or any other individual on the team. Any team member can hate country music but agree that the use of a particular country music song is good for a particular worship experience.

This is an important distinction: not that there is consensus on personally liking something, but that there is consensus that the presence of the Holy Spirit is in the idea, that it is biblically and theologically sound, that it is connected to something culturally important and resonant, and that it has creative and stylistic appeal to many in the congregation.

Methods for Making Team Decisions

Teams that work somehow find ways to give up personal agendas and achieve consensus. Ego, personal preference, position, and even seniority are checked at the door. Successful teams focus on the one central agenda of finding the best way to communicate the gospel for whatever particular topic is being discussed. Each and every member of the team must be willing to make the team's agenda more important than his or her own. Kris Melvin on the Trietsch team acknowledges this is an area to work on:

> When we walk into the team meeting, we should check egos at the door. Every idea that comes up in the meeting is everyone's idea. We need to feel free to just throw ideas out and let everyone grab a hold of them and run with it. Just because we use one person's idea doesn't mean we don't like you. It just means that there is another idea that the team felt better to run with. It is nothing personal.

Eliminate the gatekeeper mentality

The goal is not to be a gatekeeper on personal style and preference. Representatives of every ministry area, including music, media, preaching, and beyond, have to be willing to let others in on the creative development of their own particular area of expertise. In other words, a graphic artist doesn't decide which visual ideas make it through the gate. The team debates the merits and demerits of each visual idea. The group then, hopefully, comes to consensus based on what best suits the worship experience's direction (not what best suits the graphic artist's aesthetic tastes). It means music ministers allow others to participate in song selection and that pastors are aided in the development of the sermon. Each and every aspect of worship becomes open for discussion for each and every person in the room.

The role of the individual team members then becomes more about leading the discussion around a particular aspect of worship (such as music), rather than dictating what idea will become the final decision for worship.

This can be difficult for dominating personalities and for those in long-established roles such as preacher and music director. These positions have been lone ranger positions for so long that it may be extrachallenging to begin to allow others to participate in the process.

We have been involved with teams where a particular voice was so strong that it drowned out others in the room. Without a countervoice or voices against which an idea can be tested, the quality of worship suffers. Say, for example, someone on the team likes candles. This person has strong vocal opinions on why they are theologically good and why they are aesthetically nice, and even does a good job of making pretty candle displays every week. Other team members, tired of fighting the weekly assault, allow Candle Person to do his or her thing. At first the congregation is moved by the beautiful candle displays. But over time, candles...Get. Really. Old.

Related to this problem is the opener question. We often hear in consulting sessions about congregations that struggle with the beginning of worship—doing something creative while at the same time getting people's attention to start corporately. The solution is to never do the same thing until it gets predictable. Make each week of worship a surprise for those attending and you won't have any problem getting people in their seats and paying attention. Artistic tastes vary. This is true both in your congregation and on your team; so a feeling of surprise and anticipation are important. And the only way in which unpredictability can be fostered is in a team environment where multiple voices are heard with respect. Don't allow one or two voices to dominate. Remember that everyone on the team may not be in love with the themes, metaphors, images, prayers, songs, and so forth for a weekend—the more variety, the better. True consensus means losing personal agendas and agreeing that a concept is good for the gospel and good for your own unique congregation. Every aspect of worship can benefit from creative collaboration. With Christ as the head, we can become the body in a new and fresh way. Worship can only get better as a result.

Silence doesn't equal consent

There may be silent toxins growing on the team. In the case of Candle Person, others on the team may be growing to dread and abhor candles, yet feel powerless to speak up. The best antidote, while it may be a challenge to implement, is to ensure that everyone has a voice and feels free to speak his or her mind. For extroverted or talkative team members, discerning their opinion is relatively easy. It is more difficult to draw out the true feelings of quieter team members. This may require specific feedback requests: "Quiet media guy, what do you think? Tell us your honest opinion." Only when everyone vocally agrees that the idea is good for the congregation and the direction of worship can there be true consensus.

Consider a team-developed purpose statement

This idea may sound passé to some, but consider creating a mission or purpose statement for your team. A true purpose statement helps define what the team's objectives are and how they will be carried out. The more specific the purpose statement is, the better off the team will be in moving from a group of agendas to one central agenda.

The purpose statement can be an invaluable tool when conflict arises. One worship design team Len worked with experienced this firsthand. Taking the assignment of a mutually agreed-upon purpose statement seriously, they spent portions of their first six meetings together formulating a series of statements. Once they all signed the document, the team's scribe posted it with a piece of tape on the meeting room's wall. A few months later the team found itself in the middle of a serious disagreement. After extensive and heated debate, one of the team's members reached over to the original document, pulled it from the wall, and calmly began to read its contents. The solution to the disagreement became clear in light of the team's stated and agreed-upon purpose.

As stated in the quiz, all teams have either (a) experienced conflict, (b) are currently experiencing conflict, or (c) will experience conflict. There's just no getting around it: conflict is an inevitable part of working with other people. In fact, a group of individuals doesn't really move toward becoming a team until they've weathered their first conflict together. If a purpose statement is given proper attention when it's written, and is signed by every member with no reservations, it becomes a roadmap for dealing with any situation that may arise.

Purpose statements should be written over the course of several meetings. They should be as specific as possible. Each and every person on the team should be a part of writing the statement, and should be able to sign his or her name to it when completed.

A word of warning: conflict may arise even as a purpose statement is written. Use the conflict to help define even further what the goals of the team are.

Joint ownership, not best friends

When teams successfully move from individual agendas to a single agenda and discover the possibilities of consensus, many wonderful things happen. Brainstorming becomes less tense, camaraderie and mutual respect grow, and joint ownership over the process is felt. Joint ownership makes each individual feel more like a part of a team. A general excitement begins to accompany the process when everyone feels as though they're a part of what is being achieved.

This doesn't mean that everyone on the team is the closest of friends. As stated, personal styles and preferences may vary. It does mean that the team operates out of mutual respect and agreement that the decisions being made are the best ideas for worship in its own unique time and space.

Use "we" not "I" language

One important change to make is in the language used to describe the process. *We* becomes a very important word. Since the creative process is pretty messy, it's often hard to remember who said what when. One might have spawned ideas that come from another. Keeping track of who thought of what is an egocentric minefield that is sure to destroy the team.

This is where *we* becomes so important. Walking out of a team meeting and using the word *I* to talk about certain aspects of the design process can do a lot of damage to others on the team. Other unused brainstorms underpin nearly every idea that is implemented from a design team meeting. That makes the "final" idea something that was jointly achieved.

In our own ministry at Midnight Oil, we have trained ourselves to say "we" when talking about our work, even if there is a clear distinction in our own minds as to which one of us implemented any given idea. We've learned that one can lose a lot by saying "I," but we can't lose anything at all by saying "we." In fact, we can gain a lot by saying "we" when team is involved.

There is power in the body of Christ. We can do so much more together than we can alone. For the sake of the world, we must function as the body if we want to make disciples of Jesus. It's time to throw out our egos and learn to make decisions as a team.

CHAPTER ELEVEN

THE WEEKLY LIST OF DECISIONS

As aeronautics matured and longer flights began taking place, the need to predetermine flight paths, refueling stops, and safe landing zones became a priority. Pilots began to create what is now standard procedure: the flight plan.

As worship designers, there are many decisions to be made so that worship may soar. Design team meetings provide an opportunity to create a flight plan so that everyone is on the same page and headed in the same direction.

Ideally, at the conclusion of every worship team session, members should be able to clearly state each of the following for every worship experience they design:

- The text—the primary scripture on which worship is based
- The main idea—the single, central theme, derived from the text, that is the driving concept for everything in worship
- The human condition—the real-life issue of the congregation, which the big idea addresses
- The visual metaphor—the visual image that captures the big idea and connects it to the congregation
- The title—the title of the service
- The goal—What is the team trying to accomplish by this service?
- . . . and some creative elements

Various teams can accomplish this list to varying degrees of depth and complexity depending on the meeting schedule. A team representing a medium-to-large church that meets every week should be able to identify each of these elements at the conclusion of every meeting. However, a team that meets once a month or less and serves a small church would do well to create an outline sketch of these concepts for an entire series over the course of a single meeting.

So what do these elements mean? Let's analyze each in a bit more detail.

The Text

What is the primary scripture on which this service is built? Each service needs to have a primary text, or, if multiple texts are being used, the service should be built carefully around a single, unifying truth. While recognizing that different preachers have different homiletical approaches, we'd recommend a single text if possible, which gives the subsequent decisions more clarity.

The Main Idea

What is the single, central theme derived from the text that is the driving concept for every element in the service? The main idea is something that can be stated in a sentence or two. If it takes you more than that to explain your main idea, narrow your scope or clarify what you mean. The idea has to be clear and concise.

Dave Ferguson, pastor of Community Christian Church of Naperville, Illinois, wrote an entire book on this subject, fittingly titled *The Big Idea*. He states, rightly, that the presence of many small ideas in the life of a church get in the way of a single big idea. For example, Jesus said, "Follow me." A big idea, certainly; simple to understand, yet difficult to implement.

Big ideas aren't "deep teaching," that is, they are not detailed expository, doctrinal, or propositional approaches to scripture, as one would expect with a more modern approach to proclamation. Although expository teaching certainly has its place in the life of a congregation, it is also a reflection of an empirical approach that no longer has connection with many in society. For many, it becomes just that much more information to process in an already information-saturated world. Information alone doesn't usually equate to transformation. It just becomes mental gymnastics. Big ideas, rather, are clear. As Ferguson states, "Big ideas are simple, but not easy."[1]

George Will captured the same concept in describing the traits of effective leadership. In a panel discussion on Ronald Reagan, he stated, "The key is to understand the economy of leadership: you should have ideas, and they should be clear, but most of all they should be few—three at the most. [For Reagan they were] re-arm the country, cut the weight of government, and win the Cold War."[2] Will argued that every decision Reagan made drove toward one of these three core concepts, which is what made him effective. He understood the main idea.

A service can be absent a strong visual metaphor but still work if there is a single main idea and everything moves toward that one idea. This is a shocking statement to those who know us well. But the point is that a single theme is the basis for an effective metaphor (we'll discuss metaphor later).

One church Len consulted with struggled with what he called "layers of influence." Every week it seemed there were multiple elements to somehow combine into a cohesive whole: Commissioning the group going on a mission trip to Africa. Giving honor to the young man coming back from Iraq who had been told he'd be a part of the service. Giving a nod to the holiday. Raising money for the new memorial. On and on it went. The pastor developed a staff reputation (this was a compliment) as "Segue Man" because of his ability to verbally transition from one element to the next. But this ability, while impressive, did nothing to address the lack of a central, unifying focus for the service. The result was often a lack of any kind of powerful connection for the congregation. They would walk away unmoved, ready for lunch. Better than a good segue is one well-developed theme. The best way to remove these layers of influence is to centralize worship decisions through the team, or at least through a team representative.

Consider again Jesus' use of parables. Parables are concise. They have a single idea. The narrative and details flow to the point of comparison. Sometimes Jesus tells the meaning at the end, sometimes he asks questions, and sometimes he offers no interpretation at all. (This last option is frightening for many people.) And the best part of all? Parables were Jesus' exclusive mass-communication style. He understood the power of the main idea.

Extending the main idea beyond worship

It's no secret we live in an information-saturated world. Most of our congregants surf the Internet; listen to talk radio; read blogs, books, newspapers, and magazines; and watch television. But acquiring information and cultivating wisdom are separate things. On the contrary, too much information, too many ideas, can create a malaise and lead to a sort of paralysis where we feel unable to do anything.

When someone comes to church on Sunday morning and receives different messages through our song choices, our testimonies, our prayers, and our sermons, they get a case of the information age blues. They don't know how to apply everything at once, and their spiritual lives stay stuck in neutral.

At our first local church, once we had mastered the concept of a single theme in worship, in the latter part of our tenure we began to explore the idea of expanding that theme throughout the entire ministry of the church so that the big idea presented in worship would be continued in discipleship classes, cell groups, and the like.

One weekend stands out in particular. We used the metaphor of an ancient, nomadic tribe to communicate the role of Jesus followers in carrying the power of the Holy Spirit into the world. In a nomadic tribe there was always a single person whose job was to be the fire carrier. He had to carefully wrap the hot embers of the old fire in leather and bring them to the new campsite so that a new fire could be created. If the embers were to go cold, then the entire tribe could suffer. The fire carrier's role was of utmost importance. It was even more important than protecting his own family.

We started worship with a scene from the movie *The Edge*, in which a small plane crashes into a lake in Alaska. A shivering character, played by Alec Baldwin, emerges from the water and must use a flare to light a fire so he and the character played by Anthony Hopkins don't freeze. The clip led immediately into a live performance of the chorus of "Fire" by the Ohio Players. (Only the chorus was used, since the verses introduced some other, inappropriate ideas.) A two-minute original video clip explaining the fire carrier followed, and then moved into a spoken-word call to worship that summarized the theme. By the conclusion of this nine-minute opening segment, everyone in the congregation knew exactly what the main idea was. The preacher, as he liked to say, was at the one-yard line. All he had to do was trip, and he could still score a touchdown.

The result was that people took the moniker of "Fire Carrier" on themselves as Christians out in the world. People began to post with it on the church's online forums, calling one another "Fire Carrier Dan" or "Fire Carrier Betty."

Can you imagine the impact your ministry will have once it begins to harness the main idea and narrowly focus all available media to a single idea at a time? Someone can hear a single idea in worship, presented through a variety of powerful forms. She will hear the same idea in more detail when she goes to her education and discipleship classes (like the disciples coming back to Jesus in Mark 4:12, even though they didn't understand the parable of the sower). She will have an opportunity to dwell on the idea throughout the week and give feedback and discussion on it in her small group session. She can log on to the church website and read devotions, follow links, and comment on blog posts related to the main idea.

Of course, this kind of radical concept requires some serious evaluation of the church's organizational process. Ferguson suggests identifying big ideas for the coming year, and then creating an open brainstorming meeting where representatives of each ministry area are present to flesh out how the big idea will be extended into their own work. This is collaborative curriculum planning, and it has the power to transform a local congregation by allowing people to understand, retain, and live a single aspect of spiritual formation at a time.

The Human Condition

In our initial team experience at Ginghamsburg, we called this the "felt need." This was a controversial term, to some degree (not among ourselves, because we understood the intent behind the concept, but among visitors who sometimes expressed concern about a consumerist approach to proclamation). "Human condition" may be a more theologically appropriate way to describe the same thing.

Whatever term you wish to use, the key question is, What is the real-life problem facing our congregation, which the main idea addresses and to which the gospel is the solution? It can be a current event, such as higher gas prices or the state of the stock market, or a deep-seated fear such as loneliness and isolation. The human condition is something that applies to everyone, believer or not. (Incidentally, a focus on the human condition is one of the reasons we reject "seeker versus believer" as a false dichotomy in worship planning. We all live in the same world and face the same fundamental human issues, Christian or not.)

Good clues to the human condition are everywhere. For example, a recent edition of *Relevant* magazine[3] showed the results of a reader poll asking the question, "Which of the following do you struggle with most?"[3] One might assume the majority of the respondents are Christians, yet the answers look similar to what one might see in a secular magazine like *Cosmopolitan*:

- 27% Materialism
- 24% Apathy
- 21% Disconnectedness
- 21% Disillusionment
- 7% Entitlement

Contrast these with the main ideas of true wealth, purpose, community, hope, and humility.

A nuanced understanding of the congregation is vital to this element of the design process. The team must know the hopes and fears and the daily lives of its community, including both those inside the church walls and those in the outside community. At Trietsch Memorial United Methodist Church, Len's team talks often about the "Flower Mound mind-set," the realities of living life in Flower Mound, Texas, an upper-middle-class suburb of Dallas. They talk about the television show *Desperate Housewives* and the myths of prosperity and domestic perfection that, for example, have likely played a role in the numerous suicides among the student body at the high school across the street.

At Trietsch, some of the best weekends of worship are those in which the team has most effectively identified and addressed the human condition or felt need. Alan Miles, director of media at Trietsch says:

> I think we have done some cool implementation of theme and metaphor to communicate the gospel message in a relevant way. Sometimes, the messages have seemed to get at the heart of the felt need of the congregation. In those times, we have seen an impact through responses to those messages. When there is a single-focused felt need that we are working toward, we tend to communicate it clearly and effectively.

It's important to acknowledge that in your congregation, regardless of its size, a single identified "felt need" is not going to address everyone's human condition. There's a story for each person in the room. This should not diminish its importance, however. Identifying felt needs forces us to continually ask ourselves the "So what?" question. Why does this matter? What part of our brokenness does this word from God address? How does this minister to people in their places of hurt, loneliness, and desperation? It keeps the team connected to the congregation and prevents the team from navel-gazing—designing themes out of a narcissistic tendency to assume that our stories, while real, are going to reflect others' stories.

One way to maximize our connection to the congregation's felt needs is to increase team diversity, as discussed earlier. Variety in ages, genders, races, and cultural and political viewpoints can make for lively and even heated discussions, but it also serves the purpose of keeping identified human conditions close to what is actually happening in the congregation. Try to make the team a cultural microcosm of the congregation, and even the community at large.

Balancing scriptural truth with felt need

Many preachers struggle with the tension between presenting the truth as discovered in Scripture and the spiritual needs of the congregation.

An effective homiletical approach to this culture may not follow the linear path, set forward in seminary for so many pastors, of text-exegesis-application-illustration.[4] Rather, effective preaching may instead start with an exegesis of the human condition followed by a comparison to an exegesis of scripture, compared to an exegesis of image. Whereas the former developmental strategy is linear, the latter is circular and requires the careful balancing of all four elements: scripture, human condition, application, and image.

It is possible to be both faithful to the text and real to the congregation. This is why we prefer the term "human condition" to "felt need." Prophetic preaching proclaims what people need to hear, not what they want to hear, and the idea of a "felt" need implies that people are just getting a feelings fix. However, being faithful to the text without addressing how it meets people's life needs is being unfaithful to the calling of proclamation. Good worship design, like a good sermon, serves to do both.

The human condition is a statement that identifies the brokenness of the congregation, for which the gospel is the healing balm. It could be fear, or the inability to trust. For a wealthy congregation, it could be the sin of chasing after the phantoms of prosperity. Sometimes people know their own limitations. Other times, individuals in the congregation are not necessarily aware of their human condition. This is part of the challenge of good worship design. As Charles Spurgeon said, "The goal is to comfort the afflicted and afflict the comfortable." The human condition is to be both comfortable and afflicted at various stages and places in our lives. Jesus is the answer to each of these problems.

How to target the human condition

At Ginghamsburg we identified six common felt needs based on an article first published in *Atlantic Monthly* magazine. Our pastor Mike Slaughter indicated them in his book *Out on the Edge*[5]: belonging, love, identity, freedom, authenticity, and "possibilization." These felt needs were relevant to our congregation in the late 1990s. Yours today may have a different set. Maybe they reflect the *Relevant* magazine poll or are something completely different. Whatever you identify, though, don't let the list become a pair of handcuffs. Talk about the congregation and community. Identify individuals of the congregation (in your mind, not out loud) and think about their life situation. How does this idea address their issues? Ask yourself the "So what?" question. Why does this matter? In *Redesigning Worship,* our former Ginghamsburg colleague Kim Miller writes, "Each week in our meetings we ask ourselves, 'What is the human baggage we bring to this divine message?' "[6]

This kind of questioning requires brutal honesty among the team members. It means that we have to be willing to be honest about the areas in our lives of which we're not proud. This is one area in which the need for the team to be a small group, as stated earlier, becomes important. For example, when planning a series on family, the best worship designs may come out of some honest, healing discussion about our own family dysfunctions.

The Title

What is the name of the service? Does it both capture the truth of the scripture and do so in a compelling way? This one is a real challenge. It requires thinking like an advertiser, or even a headline writer for a newspaper. What is something that is descriptive but also hooks the culture in some way? Is it a double entendre, with cultural or personal connection as well as main idea description?

A few examples of good titles include:
- "A Beautiful Day" (on the Wedding at Cana, using wedding imagery and the U2 song of the same title)

- "Pure to the Last Drop" (using coffee as a metaphor for purity in Luke 3, with the cultural tie-in to the old Maxwell House campaign)
- "True Colors" (using the Sistine Chapel restoration as a metaphor for the vibrancy of new life in Christ, which included the 1980s song of the same name by Cyndi Lauper)

Be careful that the hook is positive, not negative, and that it is redemptive. At one church the pastor wanted to do a weekend called "Private Parts," named after what was a recently released Howard Stern movie. What if, based on the connection, congregation members decided to go see the film, which fully deserved its R rating? Be careful about the associations you make. Make sure they're redeemable.

The Goal

What is the team trying to accomplish with this service? For example, is it an invitation to relationship with Jesus Christ, a call to mission and service, or a vision for what it means to be a community of believers? It can also be for people to understand and remember a simple statement of truth that leads to personal transformation, such as, "God is faithful when we are faithful." Every service needs to have a stated outcome.

Creative Elements

Any good brainstorm should include a variety of creative ways to communicate a concept. These may range from Hollywood film clips to original drama to telling scripture via flannelgraph to an on-the-street video. The possibilities are endless. Chapter 8 of *The Wired Church 2.0* highlights twenty-one ways to creatively use media in worship. The list doesn't even include nonvisual creative elements such as spoken word and dramatic pieces.

When starting out, try to identify at least one creative element to communicate the main idea for the worship service.

The Visual Metaphor

What is the primary image that serves to communicate the big idea? We often emphasize in our speaking and writing the importance of a single visual metaphor to help people encounter God in ways that seem normal and right using a visual language with which they are familiar.[7]

Sometimes we get feedback from worship planners in our workshops that metaphor doesn't work for them. The main reason we can see that it wouldn't work is because of what our former pastor at Ginghamsburg called a "buckshot" approach. Much of worship is designed like buckshot, with themes scattered everywhere, none hitting their target. It's very difficult to have a single metaphor if you are trying to tie together many different themes. Powerful metaphors require powerful themes. It's a 1:1 ratio. A rifleshot approach, agreed on by the team, with one theme and one metaphor, can hit the bulls-eye.

With a good metaphor, like a parable, all the details are part of the narrative flow to the point of comparison. The details of a parable proper are not meant to have independent significance, so all unnecessary actions are omitted. The details provide a backdrop to the essential meaning of the parable. There is a "picture part" (the portrayal) and a "reality part" (the truth being expressed), which are interrelated.

If metaphor doesn't make sense or isn't a part of your team's scope, then try to brainstorm a consistent visual treatment or design for the service. Even if the images don't directly correspond to the text, they at least need to be consistent.

Bringing It All Together

A recent series at Trietsch called "Use Me" focused on service. The overall metaphor for the three-week series, which was based on the body of Christ image from 1 Corinthians 12, was music. Although Paul's metaphor is interesting, the feeling of the team was that a contemporary and visual representation of body parts might get uncomfortable or creepy. So the decision was made to use a metaphor of musicians in a symphony, each with a vital part to play. Here is a rundown of the elements for the series:

Week 1

Title: "What Part Do You Play?"

Scripture: 1 Corinthians 12

Overall concept: exploring

Main idea: To truly serve is not an act of guilt or compulsion but an act of calling and passion.

Metaphor: orchestra

Image: musical montage and instruments

Human condition: the need for meaning and purpose

Goal: motivation to explore gifts and passions

Creative elements:
- Series overview graphic image with musical elements
- Looping background video similar to series graphic
- Interview video clip for sermon walkup
- *Mr. Holland's Opus* video clip: the band's first attempt at playing, which stinks
- *Mr. Holland's Opus* video clip: a young clarinet player struggles while practicing and says she just wants to be good at something
- Theme setup with script and musical tie-in piece

Theme setup script (following clarinet player's struggles):
Don't we all just want to be good at something? Some of us are fortunate enough to be happily focused, doing the thing we know we are meant to do, in home, at work, and at church. But many of us are just mumbling and stumbling through life.

This week we're starting a new series called "Use Me." The big idea of the series is the notion that God wants us to find fulfillment—and to grow God's kingdom at the same time—by doing whatever it is we're supposed to be doing.

It's like the Apostle Paul says in 1 Corinthians 12. Each of us is a part of the body of Christ. Or, each of us has a part in the symphony of God's kingdom. Each of us is good at something. When we figure out what that is, our melodies create a God-breathed harmony from the discord of life.

This morning we're going to explore what these gifts and passions are. What part do you play? Let's worship together.

Week 2

Title: "Tune It Up"
Scripture: 1 Corinthians 12

Overall concept: equipping

Main idea: Learning to play means refining our God-given calling and passion through the work of the Holy Spirit and the tools of the church.

Metaphor: music—rehearsal

Image: tuning fork

Human condition: knowing what to do with our passions and the things that motivate us

Goal: to encourage people to connect their passions to ministry and to begin to "practice" their gifts and passions

Creative elements:
- Graphic image of musical instruments with tuning fork
- Animated introductory video setting up theme
- Mr. *Holland's Opus* video clip: Holland using "Louie Louie" to teach the young clarinet player that it's about more than notes on a page
- Mr. *Holland's Opus* video clip: Holland teaches the drummer to find his beat (montage over Stevie Wonder song)

Theme setup script (following band's first rehearsal):
Today we continue our series "Use Me." We're looking at what it means to discover our God-given passions and to use them to find fulfillment—and to grow God's kingdom—at the same time.

It's one thing to pick a part to play, as we discussed last week, but another thing altogether to learn to use it. We're not meant to play alone, without adequate guidance and instruction. That's the job of the church—to put the right people in the right place at the right time—to transform lives. When that happens, we as the community of Trietsch won't be able to contain the power of our lifesong.

So this week we say, "Tune it up!" Let's discover how we can train our hearts and be trained by the church to play with passion and make beautiful melodies for God's kingdom.

Words for coming out of "Louie Louie" clip:
Playing music is *supposed* to be fun. Serving the church is *supposed* to be fun. Somewhere in the song, though, things get out of tune. We have learned to think of volunteering as a duty, a drudgery to endure. Service is not just the notes on a page.

Words for going into the Stevie Wonder clip:
Pick up an instrument. Take the risk and play some music. If you put yourself out there, the Holy Spirit will respond in you, and we as the church will do our best to equip you, to play your unique God-given part with passion. The Holy Spirit will give you the beat and you can begin to move in rhythm with God's symphony. And the music we can create will be amazing beyond measure.

Week 3

Title: "The Master Conductor"

Scripture: 1 Corinthians 12

Overall concept: empowering

Main idea: When we play out of our passions, God empowers us to transform others' lives and at the same time brings harmony to the discord of our own lives.

Metaphor: orchestra

Image: Master Conductor graphic

Felt need: the need to find extraordinary purpose and meaning in our service activities

Goal: to know the transformative power of the Holy Spirit in our ordinary acts of service

Creative elements:
- Graphic image of a conductor with his baton ready for the downbeat
- *Mr. Holland's Opus* video clip: the end of the film, when Holland is surprised with a symphony that plays his song. In the clip, the former clarinet player, now Governor, tells him the students he served are the melody of his life.
- Original interview video clips of Trietsch members who have experienced the transforming power of service

Theme intro script:

Today we conclude our series "Use Me." We've explored our part in God's symphony, our gifts and passions. We've been equipped to play our part. Now what?

Jesus makes his followers a promise: "You will receive power." When through the music of our service God is glorified, the Holy Spirit will use our gifts in such a way to accomplish greater things than we can even imagine.

The church, equipped and unleashed in ministry, makes beautiful music. So this morning let's tune each of our instruments for praise to the Master Conductor, who brings harmony to the discordant notes of our life.

The concept of service, which is visually abstract and creatively absent, is energized by the metaphor of music, which brings vitality and life to the concept. The interrelationship of the two draws out additional truth by allowing interesting contrast and comparison.

Each service needs to have each of these elements identified. Resist the urge to partially address them. Write down the list on your whiteboard and make sure there is understanding and consensus on each of the six. Make sure that every team member has a specific list of action items to accomplish and reports back, either live or digitally, to the team.

CHAPTER TWELVE

BRAINSTORMING

Where do great ideas come from? The answer is quite simple: brainstorming. Whether one is working alone or with a group of other creative teammates, great ideas often start with brainstorms.

As the word itself suggests, brainstorming can be as hard to predict as the weather. Sometimes clouds hover over our creative minds, yet the downpour of refreshing ideas is slow to come. Other times, we're deluged with a flood of creativity that can practically drown us.

Brainstorming is a process about which many creative people and teams know too little. Conventional wisdom may suggest that just getting a group of people in the same room is enough to generate creativity. Like weather forecasting, though, surface simplicity (such as saying "It's hot" in the summertime) belies a deeper understanding of multiple forces at work. With a proper understanding of technique, brainstorming can become a regular part of the worship planning process that is both effective and fun.

The first thing to keep in mind is that brainstorming provides a structured environment for creativity. It's not just a rulebook to be followed, which can inhibit those with a bent toward creative thinking (who tend to not be very fond of rules). The point of this structure, which is casual, is to bring order to the chaos of creativity. This in turn allows ideas to thrive.

Here, then, are some time-tested techniques for structuring successful team-based brainstorming.

Keep the Brainstorming Team Small

As covered earlier in the chapter on team size, it is important to keep brainstorming groups to a relatively small size. Studies have shown that the most effective brainstorming groups consist of around four to seven people. Any more than that and it's hard to narrow down ideas and form consensus. Any less and it's hard to have enough minds focused to generate good ideas.

Even the Playing Field

The best creative groups find a way to check hierarchical structure at the door. No one wants to look bad in the eyes of their superiors, and brainstorming (from an ego standpoint) can be pretty risky. Creativity flows much easier when each member feels the same amount of authority to express ideas and to give input on ideas being discussed. As discussed earlier, the "flatter" the team feels organizationally, the better the brainstorming will be.

It may not be possible to organize staff positions in such a way that everyone is "flat" outside the meeting, but position and supervisory issues should be deemphasized during the brainstorming meeting. For example, the senior pastor may choose to intentionally charge someone else with managing the meeting and simply operate as one of the creative voices in the room.

Keep the Group Closed

Brainstorming can be risky business that encourages team members to expose their ideas and themselves to both praise and honest criticism. In our experience, the best balm for criticism is trust. A closed team—the same group of people, meeting together regularly—can build up enough trust and small group intimacy to allow honest critique to thrive without bruising egos too badly.

Once a closed group has learned to brainstorm together, a level of comfort begins to set in that makes the creative process second nature. When this point is reached, each team member will feel that the others in the room "have their back" and can begin to name ideas that would have otherwise remained unspoken inner thoughts.

Groups with creative honesty, if achieved, need to be protected with the utmost care. Adding just one new person to the group can change the dynamics in such a way that it makes brainstorming labored or even impossible. This may seem like a dramatic statement. Yet one new person brings to the group a lack of understanding of current team dynamics, a lack of a shared team history, and (most importantly) a lack of trust and relationship that exists between all others on the team. The result is a dramatic loss of team intimacy. This makes it hard for the "outsider," who will likely feel uncomfortable sharing ideas, and it also makes the more established team members guarded with their ideas. Established members may want to avoid inadvertently offending the new member or "looking stupid" in front of the new member when sharing what may seem to be farfetched ideas. And anything that slows down the transmission of ideas is a bad thing that leads to missed creative opportunities.

Of course, if the group is not working, it makes sense to open it up for some new creative energy, but be aware that the one or two people coming in have to form new relationships with every other person on the team. Teams in the process of adding new members should be aware that the dynamics will change once the new person or people enter the room.

No Bad Ideas

It is an oft-stated maxim of group brainstorming that no idea is a bad idea. This nugget of truth applies particularly to the early development stages of a brainstorming session. Although this rule often plays out better in theory than in an actual creative meeting, it is important to allow for "popcorn" creativity. As kernels of ideas pop in the minds of team members, they should be thrown out without concern for their legitimacy. As with popcorn, sometimes no kernels pop and other times multiple kernels pop simultaneously. This free-flowing portion of the creative process can germinate some great ideas. As Kris Melvin at Trietsch says, "Someone will come up with an idea, then someone else will take it further than the original. Having the team helps everyone flesh out the ideas."

It is key, however, that team members should not fear their popcorn ideas will be ridiculed. Good brainstorming allows the conversation to flow, even if it seems radically unfocused. A group freedom of thought is essential to new idea formation. (Having said that, it may be beneficial to have someone on the team who is good at keeping all the popcorn in the pan.)

Many teams, especially long-established teams, find it difficult to resist the urge to pass immediate judgment. This can be both good and bad in that it can make the process light and fun, but it can also potentially kill what might be a good kernel idea.

Although we recommend letting all ideas live for at least a brief moment without being shot down, it is a good idea for team members to develop thick skins. Remember that bad ideas lead to great ideas when it comes to brainstorming.

Write Everything Down

With creative ideas flying around left and right it can be easy to get lost in the creative chaos. Brainstorming requires only a few tools, and chief among them is a whiteboard or flipchart and a marker. Internet access comes in a close second.

Initially, it's a good idea to write everything down. Assign the role of scribe to someone in the meeting. This person's job is to record all creative thoughts, hopefully in some ordered fashion, so that everyone can keep track of what has been offered. For example, the whiteboard may have columns for movies, music suggestions, worship order suggestions, other creative elements, and more. Later in the meeting, as the team narrows its focus, some ideas will get crossed off while others may be added. When the meeting is complete the flipchart or whiteboard becomes the roadmap for the structure of the service.

An important note about the scribe: the person holding the marker is not the gatekeeper of ideas (writing down the ones he or she likes and omitting the rest). Nothing can be more frustrating than throwing out creative ideas only to have this marker-keeper ignore them.

Limit Brainstorming Time

When a group of creative types get together to brainstorm, there may be a tendency to lose track of time. Although brainstorming can be a lot of fun and the desire to keep going can be strong, it is best when the clock is limited. Limiting time effectively creates a funnel through which all ideas pass, leaving the team with the best stuff in the end. Having no limits makes it hard to know what the overall creative direction should be. It's important to assign someone on the team the task of being the timekeeper.

The correct amount of time may differ from team to team. Some teams find their ideal brainstorming window to be thirty minutes, while for others it can be two or more hours. The best indicator of when to limit the time is often when a series of good ideas and much creative energy begins to be followed by a series of bad ideas and little creative energy.

However, some teams, out of a desire to get things done, may want to jump on the first good idea that comes along and declare the brainstorming time accomplished. Just as there needs to be a clear maximum to the process, there also needs to be a minimum. Don't be afraid to sit together in the same room for at least fifteen minutes randomly responding to an idea.

Only Brainstorm Together

One of the best ways to kill the brainstorming process and the success of the team is to encourage prebrainstorming and postbrainstorming.

Prebrainstorming occurs when the pastor or other members of the team brainstorm on their own about the upcoming topic days or weeks ahead of time, either through informal meetings or group email exchanges. One might suspect that this would give the team a jumpstart in the meeting, but the exact opposite often occurs.

Given days or weeks to reflect on a topic, individuals tend to build up and fall in love with their own ideas. When the meeting begins, they eagerly anticipate the moment when they can unveil their groundbreaking, awe-inspiring ideas. In the meantime, they ignore and fail to give due attention to others sharing their equally groundbreaking, awe-inspiring ideas. The result is that rather than several individuals working toward the same goal, each individual works to get his or her idea to the top of the list.

Further, there is something about fresh exposure to an idea that can generate creative feedback. Contrary to perception, good ideas can come from initial reaction to concepts rather than to measured responses formulated over days.

Postbrainstorming may be even worse, especially for the morale of the team. This happens when a team member (most commonly the pastor) or members, after the meeting is finished and the team has set the creative direction, brainstorms alone or with another group of people within the church. In this circumstance, a different and sometimes entirely new creative direction for the service or series is set without the team's involvement. This essentially erases and invalidates the work that the creative team did in the meeting. It devalues the team and basically makes the earlier meeting a waste of time. Not surprisingly, team members become disillusioned and often leave feeling that their efforts to create inspiring worship aren't used or appreciated.

Make It Fun

Brainstorming novices may initially find the process of creative worship design intimidating, but they will soon learn that there is much fun to be had. New teams discover over time that this level of fun will grow. However, veteran teams may become tired of the process.

Whether building a new team or responding to potential creative burnout on a veteran team, be intentional about finding ways to inspire. Here are a few suggestions:

- Play games with a creative bent, such as Balderdash, Cranium, Pictionary, and the like. This will exercise team creative muscles in a fun and semiwork-related way.
- Fellowship together in a way the team hasn't before. Eat dinner or lunch together. Go to the movies. Visit a park or museum as a group. Go on a retreat.
- Change up the brainstorming process by throwing an object (such as a ball) around the room. When the ball is caught, the catcher has to shout out an idea immediately and then toss the ball to someone else.
- Spice up your environment. Conference rooms and classrooms aren't the most inspiring places to meet, even though they are commonly used for brainstorming meetings. Use color on the walls, hang posters, and maybe even add toys such as a Ping-Pong or foosball table to the room. Ditch the uncomfortable chairs for sofas, recliners, or beanbags.

The success of any team can ultimately be measured by how well the members can brainstorm together. It is from that process that everything else comes. Even the most creative individuals on the planet will not succeed within a creative design team if they don't first learn the process. There are countless books, games, and websites devoted to creative brainstorming. Check out your local library or search the Web for more on techniques and tips.

A WORSHIP CASE STUDY

The "Use Me" case study given in chapter 11 provides one case study of the results of worship planning, specifically in regard to the elements. The "Use Me" series was successful at integrating all of the elements into a cohesive whole. The congregation was able to wrap their hearts and their minds around the music metaphor without getting caught or stuck in it. They were able to see through its doorway to the truth of serving in the body of Christ.

Here is another example, called "Front Porch Stories," based on the looser (and therefore more challenging) concept of a six-week series on Jesus' parables. For the series, the senior pastor provided the team with a parable and a one-word concept that indicated the direction he wanted to go with the sermon. The rest of the creativity was the team's responsibility. As is often the case with a sermon series, the team struggled a bit to find a way to tie the sermons together thematically. Eventually, they settled on the concept of "Front Porch Stories" to describe the parables, because of its ties to summertime and storytelling and its nostalgic feel. The front porch makes a nice series metaphor because it is open-ended and multiple different stories, themes, and visual metaphors may be attached to it, allowing for the series to remain fresh and engaging over a six-week span.

Notice how the fluidity of the subject matter from week to week made it more difficult to create an integrated whole. The porch, which is a classic storytelling metaphor of the American South, made a good setting for individual metaphors related to Jesus' parables but put the onus on managing good images week to week that were both true to the specific parable being taught and made sense on a porch. As a result, the series had some good weeks and some not-so-good weeks.

The main image of a white rocking chair on a porch was given to the overall series and used on the bulletin cover and in all print promotion. With the front porch concept in place, the team could begin finding ways to use it in worship. The front porch lent itself to heavy use of drama throughout the series. So, whereas in other settings more video or graphic imagery might have been appropriate, this series was primarily about drama.

The first weekend's parable was of the prodigal son. We titled the service "Welcome Home." One of the most preached texts in the Bible, the parable of the prodigal son is a powerful story that is frequently portrayed without power. Because the series introduction was also a part of this service, the prodigal son's theme introduction was brief:

"Our First Front Porch Story"

What do you get when you have a pig, a happy dad, two brothers who don't get along, and a fat cow?

Well, we're going to explain it all today for you.

Welcome home as we celebrate worship today.

Here are the overview notes for the first week of the series:

Week 1

Title: "Welcome Home"

Scripture: Luke 15:11-32 (prodigal son)

Main idea: God's extravagant forgiveness

Metaphor: welcome home party on the porch

Goal: to experience God's extravagant forgiveness

Felt need: Our sins and bad decisions prevent us from experiencing reconciliation and forgiveness.

Creative elements: a drama centered on the angry older brother, who is out on the porch while the party is inside

Theme setup:

Did you ever live in a house with a front porch? Or maybe you knew someone who did. Nowadays, we get houses with concrete slabs in the front yard. Not quite the same thing.

But there was a time before central air, when as the sun set you sat out on the front porch, rocked, told stories, and drank lemonade.

And that's where a lot of problems got solved and lessons got learned.

Jesus knew the simple power of the front porch. He was a storyteller, too.

We're starting a new summer series that is going to look at six different stories Jesus told—each simple, yet powerful in its ability to capture the truth of the gospel.

Join us as we explore "Front Porch Stories."

Later in the service, the front porch became the setting for a dramatic monologue depicting the older brother's anger at the end of the story. Sound effects of a party "inside" the house played through the sound system as the older brother lamented his younger brother's foolish behavior and his father's extravagant forgiveness. Here is the script:

(make an exasperated face)

Did you hear about my brother?

He's come home.

What an idiot.

I mean, he's my brother and all, but what an idiot.

You know what he did, right? Decided he knew everything there was to know, took his half of the inheritance, and took off. Gone a long time, spent it all on God knows what—women, parties, liquor. (*shake head, trail off*)

So, he blows it all, and ends up sleeping and eating with pigs—literally. Now he's back home.

What an idiot.

Dad says I should be happy. Man, he was emotional. How can I be happy when he gives my brother the clothes off his back and throws a big ol' massive extravagant party in his honor? To celebrate his shame? I mean, did he have to kill the fattened cow?

All the years I have served Dad faithfully. Never said a word. Certainly never blew his money. But did he ever throw a party in my honor? (*shake head*)

(*sarcastically*) Welcome home.

(*walk off*)

At the close of the sermon, the pastor told a true story, originally told by Alexander Campbell, founder of the Disciples of Christ, of a young man returning to his family home. Three years earlier he had left in anger and hadn't spoken to his father since. Scared of his father's wrath and disapproval, he had written his mother asking them to tie a bed sheet to the family tree near the train station if his father was willing to see him. As Campbell tells the story, when the train rounded the corner to the station, there was a bed sheet tied to every branch on that tree and on every tree within sight. The entire meadow was covered in white.

After this story of extravagant forgiveness, the band played the hit song "Home" by Daughtry ("Softly and Tenderly" for the traditional service) and the congregation was invited to the altar to pray and pick up a strip of white cloth as a reminder of God's extravagant forgiveness. That weekend some in the congregation couldn't get to the altar because of all the people kneeling in prayer.

Other weeks had varying degrees of effectiveness. A fishing metaphor connected the parable of the Pharisee and the publican from Luke 18:9-

14 to Father's Day, when two men with fishing rods sat on the porch and swapped fish tales in "The Big Fish." A mom and her daughter rocked and discussed how difficult it is to wait, referring to the parable of the weeds and the wheat from Matthew 13:24-30, while some fruit ripened in a basket on the front porch in "Just Wait." In "Real Power," three children set up a lemonade stand next to the porch to raise money for a mission trip, connecting the parable of the sheep and the goats from Matthew 25:31-40 to the idea of biblical power and a church commissioning of a mission team to Mozambique. On the Fourth of July, "A Generous Nation" explored the definition of radical generosity, as Christians and as a nation, by tying the parable of the generous landowner from Matthew 20:1-16 with an image of American flags on a row of front porches. Last, "Erasing Boundaries" pulled out from the porch to look at the whole house and the fences we erect that prevent us from caring for others, as portrayed in the parable of the good Samaritan in Luke 10:25-37.

An analysis of the series reveals some highs and lows. The team agreed that the initial week ("Welcome Home") was the best, because of its strong connection to the human condition of loneliness and the need for acceptance and reconciliation. The team also liked the lemonade stand and the generous nation themes—both cases in which the front porch had a meaningful connection to the metaphor of the parable and did not simply provide a surface level connection or backdrop to the parable.

The first weekend was also the most effective because it most closely married a scripture text, main idea, image, and an aspect of the human condition. It is no coincidence that this first weekend was brainstormed in a creative flash at a staff lake house retreat. The team got away from its usual workaday environment and discovered a compelling worship experience.

As for aspects needing improvement, while the front porch was an effective setting for a variety of parables of varying subject matter, the worship team got tired of being creatively handcuffed to dramas on the porch every week. This was attributed to the length of the series moreso than the porch metaphor. As a result, the Trietsch team has decided to limit future sermon series to four weeks.

Further, some weeks, such as the week with the ripening fruit metaphor, married the text to a main idea and a metaphor but did not have a strong tie to an aspect of the human condition. Although the explanation of the weeds and the wheat and the concept of patience were intellectually interesting, they never moved beyond information to transformation. Don't expect every weekend to soar—flying is not easy.

PART FOUR

GROUNDED

Dealing with Team Maintenance and Problems

Teams that struggle with taking flight often deal with the same basic issues. Based on our firsthand and consultative experiences, let's explore some of the primary reasons teams have trouble taking flight.

CHAPTER FOURTEEN

SOLE PROPRIETOR PREACHERS

Help! My pastor won't plan ahead!" This may be the most commonly voiced complaint we hear. At some point a lost and alone creative person will make a plea for help. He or she will acknowledge the power of creative worship in facilitating transformative experiences of God; pledge an undying devotion to proclaiming the gospel through powerful images, music, and other connectional pieces; and read, train, and work to become proficient at their craft. Yet they are powerless to actually do anything because the boss leaves sermon notes an hour before worship.

What does one do when stuck with a pastor or boss who has no interest in preplanning, no understanding of the power of team development, and seemingly no respect for the work that goes into creating media for worship?

The following are a few suggestions for overcoming this problem. Some of these come from our personal experience, some from other people who have been in the same situation, and some are just theoretical. Quitting is not one of them.

Demonstrate, Don't Debate

Or show, don't tell. We talk about this in *Digital Storytellers*,[1] but it is worth saying again.

Many pastors aren't antagonistic to the power of media in worship; they're ignorant. Pastors simply want to communicate the gospel, as one pastor reiterated to us recently during a seminar. Most have been trained in seminary, even implicitly, to believe that communicating the gospel in worship is only done through the spoken or written word. Many have never witnessed God's presence in worship with images or other creative experiences as the primary medium, so they don't understand the power of visuals to communicate the word of God. If they were to be made to understand that it is possible to communicate the gospel through visual media, then most would jump at the chance to utilize an additional medium in their stockpile.

This means as an advocate of visual media and creativity in worship, it is your responsibility to provide an opportunity through which your pastor and anyone else who needs to know can experience God in a new way. One effective demonstration will do more than untold amounts of describing. It must be seen to be understood.

There are a few ways to get this demonstration going:

Ask permission

One pastor friend had a similar predicament. He was the pastor, but the power structure of his church was the small group of lay leaders. He wanted desperately to begin creative worship at his small, mainline congregation in New England. Knowing they would resist any creative element he just sprang on them one Sunday morning, he decided to ask permission from the lay leadership to do something different one Sunday. He said, "I'd like to do something creative with the worship service and the sermon. It will be on the parable of the mustard seed. I'd like to do this on Sunday, November 7. Will you humor me with this?"

Of course, such a nice plea demands a yes. So, he diligently prepared and conducted his creative service with forethought and excellence. (It wasn't anything huge—a movie clip and a dramatic interpretation of the scripture reading. But it was huge to the congregation.) Afterward, he went back to the usual way, to allow any furor to subside, and then a few months later he asked permission again. Continuing on this way, he managed to increase the frequency from once a quarter to once a month to now, after two years, weekly worship. By the way, attendance has increased.

Consider youth-led worship

Often youth pastors are very open to the use of media to present their messages and will be more than happy to plan ahead to incorporate it into the service. This gives you and your youth minister a chance to make a lasting impression on the church and staff, and to provide a leadership opportunity for your youth.

Adults love to see their children and grandchildren excited about their faith, so it's a good bet that they'd happily receive a youth-led media service. If your church doesn't do this on a regular basis, start taking steps to make it happen. Although once a year is better than never, hopefully a creative presentation of the gospel in worship will also connect with the pastor, who then will show interest in some of the same methods in his or her own planning.

Target a special-event service

Another opportunity is the twice-a-year, big holiday, or "special" Christmas and Easter services, which are statistically the two highest-attended services annually. Many churches are aware of the large numbers of "C and E" people (attendees who only come twice a year) and do some degree of preplanning to take advantage. Consider incorporating visual elements into these services to take advantage of existing preplanning and, because the services are a good ministry opportunity to infrequent attendees, to demonstrate media to those staff and lay leaders who would support reaching them.

During the preplanning stages for these "event" services, infuse every meeting with discussions of how visuals and metaphors might be incorporated into the service. Use holiday weekends as an opportunity to raise the bar. Once you've set a new standard, it will be hard to go back.

In addition to Easter and Christmas, try doing something special for Mother's Day (statistically the third-biggest-attendance week of the year), Father's Day, Memorial Day, Baptism Sunday, September 11, Graduation Sunday, and more. Just seeing how media adds to these special occasions can help bring about change on the rest of the weeks of the year.

Use a visiting preacher

If your church participates in a pulpit exchange program with other churches in the area, you might try working with the visiting pastor in the weeks leading up to his or her sermon at your church. Pulpit exchange weeks create an environment to experiment with the way worship is done.

Design media after the service is complete

This one sounds a little crazy and as though it could potentially be a lot of wasted effort, but it might work miracles with your pastor. Sit through worship one weekend and take careful, detailed notes about how visual media might be incorporated. If possible, set up a camera to record the entire service, or if your church already does IMAG (image magnification), obtain a copy of the feed after worship.

With your notes in hand and maybe the IMAG feed to watch, gather a group of people who share your vision for working in team to design a metaphor or some other type of visual direction for the service. In other words, brainstorm after the fact. Pay close attention to scripture references and sermon illustrations and then find visuals that tell the same story.

When your "postservice" design team finishes its meeting, develop the media as you would for the actual service. If you are capable of doing so, edit the graphics (and maybe even video clips) into the service as if they were there during the live event. Give yourself a week or two to completely finish your retrofitted media service, keeping in mind that this first impression will be important.

Finally, schedule a meeting with the pastor where you can sit down and view the visually rich service in its entirety together, or at least view the graphics you have created for it. Prior to starting the video (if you're going that route), share the vision you have for making the visual aspects of worship stronger. Explain that what he or she is about to see is a demonstration of your hope for what might happen with a week or two of lead time, and then thank your pastor for his or her openness to these ideas. Throughout the viewing interject thoughts about how things might be accomplished in a planning meeting. Highlight how stories become even stronger when matching visuals enhance them. Then give your pastor plenty of time to think about it following the meeting. Be sure to check back after some time has passed.

Request that Your Pastor Meet with Others in a Creative Team Environment

Pastors have also been trained to design worship by themselves. Many have a lonely understanding that God's word is only revealed to writers in quiet rooms surrounded by books and that to proclaim God's word one must go into isolation. In fact, the early church as outlined in Acts was a riotous atmosphere of interchange—quite different from the traditions handed down to us from monasteries and writers. Other pastors are simply very busy and don't place a high value on sacrificing time to do in a team what they think they can accomplish just as well, and with less time, on their own.

As with the use of media itself, many pastors are ignorant, not antagonistic, about the power of teams. If a pastor knew designing in teams would communicate the gospel more clearly, he or she would be all for it. One pastor Len has worked with, Joe Carmichael, had a prior, failed attempt at team-based worship design. Joe stated, "My earlier attempt was to put together what I called a message 'research' team. The goal was to design worship with a visual theme or metaphor connected throughout. However, I did not make time for face-to-face interaction but instead tried to operate via email. It didn't work. Eventually only one person was shooting me ideas."

In spite of Joe's first experience, he was gracious enough to try a second time, at Len's request. The second team has worked and the quality of worship has dramatically improved, partly because in a group setting the team does not operate as a sounding board for the pastor's preconceived worship ideas but instead understands itself as the primary design group for worship. Joe says, "I now think that an intentional meeting time, where team members gather to share ideas, sharpen their ideas, build community, and provide accountability, is essential to its success."

By being willing to sacrifice valuable time and submitting himself to the dynamics of a team to do what he formerly did on his own, Joe had a much better result. Like most pastors, Joe is highly pragmatic. He just wants to design worship that works and is open to anything that will get him there. Remember, pastors are trained in modern-era seminaries that place a heavy emphasis on books. Books—both reading them and writing them—are individual experiences. A by-product of such a book emphasis is that pastors are trained to think and work alone in their ministry.

There are multiple problems with working alone, including loneliness and busyness. One of the worst, though, is that a bad idea remains a bad idea. Most of the time lone sermon planners don't know it's a bad idea until the words spring from their mouth as they are delivering the message. That is mostly avoided in a team environment where creativity is exponential and a bad idea is a path to a good one. Learning to trust in the power of a team takes a lot of time and many small steps but results in savings of time as well as better worship.

If your pastor is not willing at first to meet with a team, then request to meet one-on-one with him or her for the purpose of creating images that will correlate with sermon points and illustrations. Working within the boundaries that already exist, no matter how tight, may provide you with an opportunity to create something that will speak to your pastor in such a way that she or he will understand the power of media and the power of team.

State Your Case in Simple Terms

Explain that preachers take time to plan, musicians don't usually practice for the first time on Sunday morning, and hosts and spoken-word people don't often just stand up and wing it. Media people must also be allowed to prepare and plan ahead so that their contributions may have the same care, devotion, and skill as any of the other elements of worship.

There is a simple but powerful concept to keep in mind if you're frustrated about not being able to preplan for worship: if you don't ask, the answer is always no. You might find that gently asking if preplanning is possible is enough to make it happen.

Have Your Pastor Write a Backup Sermon

Although this may sound facetious, we're actually being quite serious. There are many pastors who insist that God speaks to them on Saturday night—not just little things to interject, but entire sermons. We won't question the validity of this method, but sometimes wonder about who's waiting until the last minute—the Holy Spirit or the pastor. Regardless, last-minute inspiration leaves the media person or persons scrambling on Sunday morning to throw things together that often don't fit with the message. This endlessly revolving problem can be solved with one simple backup sermon.

Plead with your pastor to write one sermon ahead of time to be used at an unspecified date in the future. Once that backup sermon is in place, create media to match it. When your pastor arrives one Sunday morning, beg to use the backup sermon instead of what was delivered the previous night. If God spoke to him or her on Saturday as God usually does, there is sure to be a sermon ready for that day. Ask the pastor to shelve the sermon from the night before for one week and use that time to brainstorm and develop media around it for the following Sunday. When God speaks to your pastor on the following Saturday night, ask him or her to write it all down as if it were going to be delivered the next morning, but again to shelve it for use on the following week. Instead, use the sermon that was written for the previous Sunday. A few weeks of this and the vicious cycle will be broken.

Of course, persuading a strong-minded pastor to actually do this method might be difficult, but such a discussion might lead to other ways that media can be integrated into the sermon.

Request a Few Talking Points, Main Ideas, or Lines of Manuscript Ahead of Time

If it's just not possible to get the pastor to write the whole sermon a week to a few days early, try to get the main ideas ahead of time. The purpose of these clues is to design a central metaphor for worship.

This is not the best-case scenario, as a few things scribbled on paper don't have the ability to interact and become fleshed out during brainstorming. As we often say, "Pieces of paper don't talk," but it is a place to start. You and other team members can attempt to develop a visual thread that goes from the beginning of the service all the way through the sermon by using whatever scribbles you can get from the preacher.

The potential disaster with this method of change comes when the preacher shifts directions without telling the team or informs them too late for things to be changed. The result is a disjointed service, where visuals don't tie in. But if you are desperate for something to work with, a few lines of text may be better than nothing.

Design the Rest of the Worship Experience Apart from the Sermon

If none of the above suggestions equate to any development or growth for your situation, a last-ditch effort to incorporate visuals into worship may involve ignoring the preacher and focusing on the other elements of worship.

In this case, everyone involved with producing worship, including musicians, media people and artists, liturgists, and so on—but not including the pastor—brainstorm a theme together at least a week prior to the service. The theme that develops is woven together through the variety of worship elements so that the entire event, minus the sermon, communicates a common idea. The potential consequences are that the sermon could appear ill fitting by comparison and the event may come across as a worship mutiny. But it may also form a sort of de facto demonstration of the potential of visual metaphors to communicate the gospel in worship.

Last Resort, Give the Pastor a Noogie

If you resort to this method, we take no responsibility for your actions—but we'd love to know the outcome! Email us with your tragedy and we'll pass it along to others for their comfort.

Most pastors feel a strong calling to reach the lost and will do whatever it takes to get there. The idea of planning ahead or designing worship (in particular, sermon material) as a team is relatively new. A lot of pastors who are perceived to be "anti-team" have either never been asked, have never explored what that means, or have had a bad experience in the past. As creative types, we can help pastors do what they do in even more powerful ways through creativity and visual communication.

Any process of change starts with prayer, vision casting, communication, patience, and continued commitment to one another. Take a moment to explore what your pastor's thoughts are on preplanning. Chances are, once you show the benefits, he or she will be on board at some level.

MAINTAINING A FINELY TUNED MACHINE

Whereas the more interesting story at Kitty Hawk, North Carolina, in December of 1903 was, of course, the story of the first powered flight of a heavier-than-air machine, the Wright Flyer was not the only thing the brothers built at Kill Devil Hills.

Over the course of three years the brothers built and improved a small building where their aircrafts could be constructed and repaired between flights. They knew that constructing a plane wasn't enough; they'd have to continually maintain and repair their invention if they wanted to continue to fly.

Likewise, building a team is only part of the journey of ongoing creative flight. Your team will need to engage in and commit to regular diagnostics and preventative maintenance to continue to find success.

Here are some of the things that keep otherwise successful teams grounded.

Conflict Avoidance

As a team, one of quickest ways to nosedive toward the ground at a high rate of speed is to collectively avoid conflict. The inconvenient truth of worship teams that work is that they've learned to successfully manage conflict together. Like any real interpersonal relationship, the small group relationship of a team relies on the ability to address conflict as it arises.

Although very few people enjoy dealing with conflict, conflict can be a very good thing for a team if it is properly dealt with. It has the ability to better define process, motivations, and interpersonal communications. In seeing other points of view, our eyes can be opened to new possibilities. Ultimately the team is strengthened.

Wilbur Wright once said, "I like scrapping with Orv. He's such a good scrapper. We engaged in innumerable discussions, and often after an hour or so of heated argument we would discover that we were as far from agreement as when we started, but that both had changed to the other's original position in the discussion."[1] A significant part of their process was engagement in heated discussions. Their passion and ability to defend their viewpoints while remaining open to the other's position was one of the key reasons they were able to succeed where others had failed.

The ability to engage in "scrapping," as the Wright brothers did, assumes a brotherly type relationship. As discussed earlier, a high level of mutual trust and confidence in one another's work forms the basis for the ability to disagree and explore varying viewpoints. Thus, conflict usually isn't something that will rear its head until the team begins to mature. Just as in a relationship between two individuals, with shared history comes a deeper awareness of differences. Little things that were once overlooked may become big things if not dealt with in an open and honest way.

One worship design team started out flying almost from the beginning. With many early successes it took months to see that things were beginning to quietly fray and fracture under the surface. All volunteers except for the pastor, this team was made up of many passionate, committed, creative types. While the team was pretty diverse in the skill sets represented, there was overlap in the area of music. Two very talented musicians shared the "praise and worship" duties, and both were excellent at their craft.

One of the two members tended to be more timid when it came to speaking out for himself, while the other was often quick to jump on the various duties that would arise from the meeting. Over time the timid musician began to feel like his contributions to the team were being underutilized. This left him disillusioned. It wasn't long before he wore his frustration on his sleeve among the other team members.

While this was becoming apparent to other members of the group, the pastor did nothing. He was not very comfortable with conflict. Tensions continued to build. Eventually it seemed an elephant had joined the design team and was always present in the center of the room during the meetings. Still the pastor avoided the harder discussions that were necessary to resolve the conflict.

In time, the timid musician decided to leave the team because of his frustrations about the music. This hurt the morale of the team but didn't prompt the pastor and other team members to dig deep into the matters that had caused the rift. The musician's wife was also on the team in the role of producer. As de facto leader, her presence on the team gave a level of comfort and assurance that fueled the energy of the entire group. Tensions between the producer and her husband began to mount as she was still involved and he wasn't, and they decided that she should also leave her position as well. This had a devastating effect on the team.

One-half of another married couple dropped out and after nearly a month and a half the other spouse decided to leave because of household tensions like those the other couple experienced. With four members of the team now gone, it was only a matter of time before the others left too. The team dwindled from ten members to two—the pastor and his wife.

One tough, honest conversation would have likely saved that team. Within the span of one or two meetings things could have been resolved and the team strengthened. Instead, the avoidance of conflict led to a complete and total breakdown of a team that had been soaring high on a weekly basis.

Sure, it's uncomfortable, and no, it's not fun, but hard conversations can save relationships and strengthen team foundations. Being willing to deal with conflict says that the feelings of others matter. They matter enough to enter an uncomfortable place and to deal with the tough stuff that comes from facing it, rather than running away from the issues at hand. Not dealing with conflict implies to others that an issue is known and it's not worth the hurt, nerves, and ruffled feathers that will come from dealing with it. It is like saying, "I know there is a problem, but I would rather lose my position than feel uncomfortable."

The tough reality is that you almost can't say you're taking flight as a team until you've successfully managed conflict. How you deal with the worst of times and situations will have a direct effect on how well you deal with things in the best of times.

Conflict is also a litmus test for passion. Passionate people are willing to get back up from the wreckage and rebuild the plane. They're willing to face the tough stuff so that everything that follows is better than what came before.

One of the best ways to establish ground rules for conflict is by creating a mission or purpose statement as referred to in chapter 2. What the team puts on this document in the easy times becomes a roadmap for the tough times.

Control Freaks and Lone Rangers

Nearly 100 percent of the time collaboration results in something that is better than what can be done alone. Sometimes, however, it seems human nature wants us to do things on our own. It's probably ego and pride that prevent us from wanting to work with others, because when there is success in something achieved alone, the accolades funnel right down to the individual who's accomplished the feat.

We've learned in our two-person team as Midnight Oil that the feeling of individual "glory" pales in comparison to accolades that can be shared by trusted cocreators. Just as the Wright brothers shared in their achievement, we too can gain much more than the transience of individual glory by working together.

Of course, this mentality isn't automatic. For creative, educated individuals, it can be hard to permit others to participate in a process that they often feel they know the most about. As stated earlier, we call that stumbling block the "gatekeeper by expertise" mentality.

For instance, if Jason were acting as a gatekeeper by expertise in the realm of graphic arts, his pride and ownership would prevent him from hearing and truly considering the ideas of others. Instead, he would try to dominate the art discussion, making it difficult or even impossible for anyone else to contribute anything that might be used in the service. Jason likes to say that he has designed many more "teddy bear," pastel-type images for worship than he would have ever preferred, but if the direction of the team moves in that way, it is his job in the role of graphic artist to produce what the team plans, not to make individual value judgments on whether it fits his personal styles and preferences.

Each role should be assigned to help guide discussion in a particular area, not shut it down, so there can be no gatekeeper mentalities within the team. Musicians, graphic artists, and pastors alike must learn to share their area of expertise when it comes to creative input if the team is to succeed. Veto power only comes in when the team member is unable to create what the team has dreamed together. It is the team member's job to honestly assess her or his ability to create an idea, not whether she or he wants to create it. Regardless of the role, it is the job of every member of the team to represent the team's decisions to the best of his or her ability.

We've often seen this challenge with the long-established worship roles of music and preaching. In our ministry we regularly encounter churches that describe musicians as the hardest nuts to crack when it comes to the gatekeeper mentality. There is a certain territorialism about music choices and styles, personally tied to religious experience, that may make it very hard to create worship as a team.

A team will begin to fly longer and for greater distances when they begin to look at worship as one story being told in different voices. If each and every team member has the ability to fully participate in discussions not relating to their expertise, incredible things will happen.

On one team, we brainstormed music ideas with our music director (an accomplished jazz musician). Someone on the team suggested a Garth Brooks song called "Unanswered Prayers." For our hepcat jazzy friend, this was much like fingernails on a chalkboard. He was not a fan of country music in the least bit, but, believing in the team process, he said, "I'm going to trust you all on this one." That weekend the band performed the song as planned. Spontaneously and without an invitation, worshipers began to approach the altar until it was completely overtaken in an inspiring display of connection to the Holy Spirit.

The following week our music director came to our design team meeting and said, "I'm so glad for this team. Had you not pushed me to do that song, we'd have never seen what we experienced this weekend. I would have never gone there on my own. Thanks for your commitment to this process." He was right. If we become gatekeepers we miss opportunities to influence lives for God's kingdom.

Just as gatekeepers can make designing worship hard, control freaks can make implementing what is designed a painful and frustrating experience. For example, whereas every member of the team should feel ownership over the service, the worship producer is usually the person saddled with the responsibility of keeping all of the pieces in motion around one cohesive design. That's no small task. It is a small and easy step for a producer in this situation to make the shift from concern and attention toward getting all of the elements together into micromanagement.

For a creative type, there is nothing worse than being micromanaged. No artist wants to be treated as a technician or a glorified "button pusher." Be it musician, designer, video producer or writer, or any creative role, on worship teams that work, artists have permission to fulfill the team's vision within their area of giftedness while continuing to stay true to that which was set forth in the design team meeting.

In one team, the worship producer had the tendency to literally stand behind various members of the team and direct them in their craft, including a weekly visit with the graphic artist. This producer would peer over the shoulder of the graphic artist and act as a "by-proxy" designer, directing layout decisions, font choices, and other aspects of design. As one would expect, such behavior was both frustrating and demoralizing for the designer, who felt disempowered to use his gifts in ministry.

Micromanagement implies a lack of trust. It also suggests of a lack of appreciation for the skills of others. Micromanagers tend to destroy the confidence of those on the team, and this leads to poor performances in all tasks associated with worship design. After prolonged exposure to a micromanaged environment, team members may become timid, disconnected, and even creatively paralyzed.

This is not to say that artists should be given complete autonomy. There will always be course corrections along the way where it might be necessary to change a song, rework a graphic, or recut parts of a video. Often, the producer will have the big picture in mind better than anyone else, but making suggestions along the way is a far cry from treating creative individuals as trained hands to carry out one person's creative vision. The litmus test is the creative direction of the team, implemented by the vision of an expert individual.

Of course, any member of the team can micromanage. For example, pastors who have a long history of being the sole proprietor of worship design might feel uneasy about giving up control to others on the team. But we have repeatedly witnessed that pastors who are willing to empower and trust their team members will never want to return to the old way of doing worship "Lone Ranger" style.

Commitment and the Revolving Door

The Wright brothers worked for three years on their flight experiments before they ever lifted off in a powered aeroplane. They stuck to the task because they had built a comfortable and collaborative working environment.

Some teams struggle to take flight because of a commitment problem. Teams that work together, fly together. This means that staff and lay worship personnel must abandon old committee and task force models that bring together a group of people for a predetermined, limited time. In our experience, teams that take flight don't rotate their membership every year or two. They are composed of a set group of individuals with a deep commitment to the process of worship design.

To ask individuals to become involved with something that has no end date means the experience had better be fulfilling. When worship design is treated only as a task and the process is not fun, safe, and collaborative, retaining new members can become almost impossible. In this environment, when worship designers do show up, there is a sense that worship design doesn't matter much and the quality of worship being designed is poor. If team members dread the regularly scheduled meetings, the environment is not conducive to keeping members on an ongoing basis. However, when teams are functioning well, the meetings may become the highlight of a team member's week (as we have both experienced and witnessed). In this environment, they are likely to commit to being there for the long haul. The design process becomes both fulfilling and fun. Worship design improves, worship improves, and others are drawn to the process. One of the best recruitment tools for worship design teams is consistently powerful worship!

If your team is having trouble with participation, start first with team-building exercises, such as social activities (movies, miniature golf, bowling, and so on), and move toward creating safe space (as described in chapter 9).

Burnout

Getting members to show up on an ongoing basis and not take on too much responsibility is challenging. Volunteers who take on too much and don't take breaks are headed for burnout. Worship teams that aren't carefully monitoring the process may find that team members who happily signed up for the long haul in time become weary after engaging in the weekly grind of worship.

Passionate volunteers are notorious for wanting to take on as much as they can in fulfilling their calling. Unfortunately, resource-hungry churches often take advantage of such volunteers without even realizing the effect they're having on them. What starts out as a small- to medium-size commitment can quickly grow to an overwhelming time vacuum.

The signs of burnout can present themselves in many ways. Team members may become cynical, sarcastic, or overly critical at meetings. Productivity begins to slip, and when burned-out teams gather, they have trouble getting started. The energy and passion that once burned white-hot can need a lot of stoking to warm up again, and sometimes simple decisions seem insurmountable.

Of course not everyone in a team experiences burnout in unison, and the aforementioned warning signs might be exhibited in individuals as well. Being proactive about preventing burnout is extremely important if the team is to remain in the air.

Here are a few things that can help in preventing burnout:

- Change venues. Sometimes the environment is the problem. Moving to a new location can help unleash dormant creativity.
- Bring toys. Sometimes just having creative objects in the room to play around with can lighten the mood and provide idea-generating entertainment. Blocks, clay, and other creativity-inducing toys might help enliven the meetings.
- Do a group activity. Although teams should always strive to have some sort of group activity, the reality is that when things start working, extras go out the door. What once was part of the process early on is now long forgotten. Playing board games, watching movies, or setting up other "bite-sized" fun activities to coincide with meetings can be a breath of fresh air.
- Take a creative retreat. Go to a theme park or another creative place as a team and be inspired by the work of other creative individuals.
- Add new blood. Sometimes adding a new person to a team can really bring about positive change. It's risky, because someone new can have the equal and opposite reaction, but the right person can help a team see things with a new perspective. Use caution if exercising this tip!

Lack of Time

Otherwise talented and amazing teams can also stay grounded for lack of time devoted to the worship design process. The brainstorming and planning process is a time hog. Busy people in ministry (which includes everyone in ministry) may wish it weren't so, but a lack of time may be the most common cause for grounded teams, in our experience.

One team that we worked with was composed of a number of talented individuals, but struggled for a long time with taking flight. In an analysis of the "product" of worship it seemed all of the elements were present, but for some reason things weren't working. A closer examination of the process revealed that the team was moving too quickly to the structure and worship order parts of the brainstorming process. They weren't allowing concepts to grow, which in turned stifled creativity. As Len observed, "Worship at this team is half-baked. If they would only give themselves another thirty to sixty minutes of brainstorming, they'd be so much better." This team eventually realized for themselves their time problem and has made schedule adjustments to give worship planning the attention it needs.

John Allen, senior pastor at Trietsch, says that the most effective aspect of the worship team is the creative process, with the caveat, "when we give ourselves the time." At the same time, he acknowledges, "We do not allow enough time for the creative process." Musician Paul Bonneau agrees and says the key is to take advantage of team building and brainstorming retreats to foster creativity, and then to realize ideas from the retreats in week-to-week planning. The growth point for the Trietsch team, as of this book's writing, is a better grip on consistency and long-range planning.

Remember that building the aeroplane and getting it off the ground isn't the end of the journey. In order to continue to fly, the team has to enter the hanger every now and then for repair. Working with your team to ensure a proper maintenance schedule will have your team flying to unimaginable heights long into the future.

Nobody ever said taking flight with creativity in worship team planning was easy. But the rewards far outweigh the challenges. If the goal is to design worship that works—to take flight—then every step of the process behind the scenes, from team formation to process management to creative formation, is worth the trouble. We guarantee that if you ever experience the honor and privilege of being a part of a team that somehow manages to create an atmosphere through worship where people's hearts are strangely warmed, where people come to know the saving power of Jesus Christ and are in turn called to go out into the world and make disciples, all of the effort will seem like making a paper airplane in comparison.

NOTES

2. Identifying Team Purpose

1. Len Wilson with Jason Moore, *The Wired Church 2.0* (Nashville: Abingdon Press, 2008).
2. Bob Rognlien, *Experiential Worship: Encountering God with Heart, Soul, Mind, and Strength* (Colorado Springs: NavPress, 2005).

3. Addressing Issues of Methodology

1. *Microsoft Encarta Dictionary*, http://encarta.msn.com/dictionary_1861718978/temporal.html
2. Ibid.
3. Ibid.

4. Who's on the Design Team?

1. Warren G. Bennis, *Organizing Genius: The Secrets of Creative Collaboration* (Reading, Mass.: Addison-Wesley, 1997), 209.
2. Ibid., 200.

6. How Does the Team Operate? Team Equality

1. A favorite book on niche business is Chris Anderson's *The Long Tail: Why the Future of Business Is Selling Less of More* (New York: Hyperion, 2006). Another relevant read is *The Wisdom of Crowds* by James Surowiecki (New York: Doubleday, 2004), which makes the claim that, contrary to popular belief, in certain instances groupthink is actually better after all.

10. Learning to Make Decisions Together

1. http://tglips.wordpress.com/2007/02/23/consensus-vs-compromise/

264
W7498T

11. The Weekly List of Decisions

1. Dave Ferguson, *The Big Idea: Focus the Message, Multiply the Impact* (Grand Rapids, Mich.: Zondervan, 2007), 24.

2. Evan Thomas, "The Left Starts to Rethink Reagan," *Newsweek*, May 12, 2008.

3. "Seven Burning Issues," *Relevant*, May 2008, 66.

4. Adam Hamilton, Plenary address, Leadership Institute, Church of the Resurrection, Leawood, Kan., October 3, 2008.

5. Michael Slaughter, *Out on the Edge: A Wake-up Call for Church Leaders on the Edge of the Media Reformation* (Nashville: Abingdon Press, 1998), 79.

6. Kim Miller, *Designing Worship: Creating and Integrating Powerful God Experiences* (Loveland, Colo.: Group, 2004), 45.

7. For more information on metaphor see our book *Design Matters: Creating Powerful Images for Worship* (Nashville: Abingdon Press, 2006), beginning on page 23.

14. Sole Proprietor Preachers

1. Len Wilson and Jason Moore, *Digital Storytellers: The Art of Communicating the Gospel in Worship* (Nashville: Abingdon Press, 2002).

15. Maintaining a Finely Tuned Machine

1. http://www.nasm.si.edu/wrightbrothers/who/1859/wilburOrville.cfm

3 4711 00200 2725